IDEALS TO LIVE BY

Other Books by the Same Author:

THE PRIEST AT HIS PRIE-DIEU

THE NUN AT HER PRIE-DIEU

THE SEMINARIAN AT HIS PRIE-DIEU

EVERYMAN AT HIS PRIE-DIEU

SEND FORTH THY LIGHT

THY LIGHT AND THY TRUTH

MARRIAGE, BEFORE AND AFTER

LIVING YOUR FAITH

THIS IS CHRISTIANITY

WE CATHOLICS

STANDING ON HOLY GROUND

THAT THEY BE ONE

THE INCURABLE OPTIMIST

SAINT OF THE DISPLACED

Ideals to Live By

*A GUIDE TO THE SPIRITUAL EXERCISES
OF ST. IGNATIUS LOYOLA*

by

ROBERT NASH, S.J.

BENZIGER BROTHERS, INC.

New York—Boston—Cincinnati—Chicago—San Francisco

DE LICENTIA SUPERIORUM ORDINIS:
JOANNES J. COYNE, S.J.,
Vice-Praep.-Prov. Hib. Soc. Jesu

NIHIL OBSTAT:
REV. DANIEL V. FLYNN, J.C.D.
Censor Librorum

IMPRIMATUR:
✠ FRANCIS CARDINAL SPELLMAN,
Archbishop of New York,
June 15, 1959

41424

Printed in the United States of America

To
MARY
Queen and Mother
of the
Society of Jesus

CONTENTS

FOREWORD

THIS BOOK is written for the laity. Priests and religious too may, we hope, find it helpful. It may be considered suitable for retreat reading either in public or in private. It may suggest lines of development for some of the meditations given by St. Ignatius in his *Spiritual Exercises*. The pages have evolved gradually over a period of more than twenty years, during which it has been the privilege of the author to act as guide in many retreats to priests and religious, and laity in widely differing walks of life.

But it is in the main laymen and laywomen whom he has kept in mind while writing. Indeed the idea of putting these chapters together at all is the result of a letter received from a Catholic lay student extolling the power and genius of the Ignatian Exercises—the writer had made them several times—and expressing the keen desire that something might be done to make them better known.

A famous doctor who lived in Rome at the time of St. Ignatius used to maintain that whenever the saint entered the darkened room of some sick person, the room was instantly filled with a dazzling light. No one will deny our modern widespread darkness and the apparently insoluble enigmas that agitate the minds of all men. It may be asserted with confidence that the light which shone from the face of St. Ignatius has been captured in his written words where it waits to be explored.

In the long line of Popes, reaching back from our present august Pontiff to Paul III who first approved the Exercises, you will find that nearly every occupant of the Chair of Peter has eulogized the content of that little volume. St. Charles Borromeo used to say that from it he received his first impulse and his first real desire to become a saint and explicit instructions how to set about sanctity. From the same source St. Philip Neri learned to esteem contemplative prayer and a life of constant union with God. St. Francis de Sales considered that this small book had effected marvels of conversions, having saved as many souls, he would estimate, as it contains words.

"I am just as assured today as ever I was," writes Ramon Navarro, the film actor, "that life is absolutely wasted if we make it merely a material thing. For this reason, when I am overtired, and all the petty details of life seem to become mountains, I go to El Retiro (a retreat house near San Francisco) for what we call a retreat. I see no one from outside nor do I read the newspapers. Every day I listen to short talks from one of the Fathers—talks about life and death, the shortness of life, the inevitability of death, and the right way to live so as to be ready to die. This may sound rather gloomy; I do not find it so. It helps me to rediscover a sense of proportion, to realize the pettiness of the little things that trouble me. I come out into the world again feeling refreshed and assured as to the essentials of life."

Such encomiums might be multiplied indefinitely. One is aware, however, that there are those who find the book disappointing. Admittedly, Ignatius did not bother to cultivate the niceties of style. His book in large measure consists of jottings put into writing as a help to the priest who would give the Exercises to another. The value of these notes is in the ore they will be found to contain if they are used with persevering adherence to the author's instructions. This they will not yield up to the casual reader, nor even to the assiduous student. Appreciation comes in the measure in which the Exercises are lived.

This little book makes no pretense of being an exhaustive study. What it aims at is simply to expand some of the thoughts and teachings of St. Ignatius by way of illustrating how much material he can pack into a single meditation, or even into a sentence or phrase which at first reading seemed dry and uninteresting. The hidden treasure unearthed in this way should be indicative of how much still lies underneath the surface. No result of perusing these pages would delight the author more than that of provoking the reader to tap the sources for himself.

"Personal experience," writes Father Cohausz, S.J., in his *Priest and St. Paul*, "always cleaves more closely than what has been merely learned." It is this principle which gives such authority and such power to the book left us by St. Ignatius. He caters to every type of soul. He envisages souls who have squandered many of life's best years and sets himself to rouse them from their state of spiritual slumber. He is much concerned with those souls who want to refuse God nothing. To these he speaks from the book of personal experience about what he has learned of the ineffable dealings of God with those who put no limits to their generosity. He wrote four hundred years ago with the vision of a twentieth-century psychologist.

Whatever worth may be in these few pages, they derive it in the measure in which they succeed in becoming and continuing to be a faithful echo of the master's voice.

I

THE GOLDMINE

IF you break your arm it is going to be quite stiff even
after the bone has knitted again. When you take it
out of the sling you find difficulty in writing or playing
tennis. You are out of practice. If ease of movement is
to be restored you will have to exercise the muscles.

You may have a talent for languages. Once upon a
time, perhaps, you spoke a foreign language fluently.
But you lost interest. You let your talent lie fallow and
all that is now left to you is a mere smattering.

It is just the sort of thing that is happening to men's
minds today. For want of exercise, they have become
atrophied. Or if men do use them, it is to employ them
almost exclusively in the study of what falls under the
experience of the senses with no reference to God. The
machine perhaps is very nearly perfected, but is it at
the price of leaving man himself in a sorry state of under-
development?

Sooner or later every man must learn that the craving
in his mind for knowledge can be satisfied only by the
supreme truth that is God, that the thirst in his heart
for happiness only the love of God can assuage. Most
men have run away from this basic fact. They have for-
saken the fountain of living water and have dug for
themselves cisterns, broken cisterns, which can hold no

water. For the want of exercise their minds no longer
take any interest in the study of God, and their hearts,
coated over with rust, remain irresponsive to the appeals
of His love.

These realities, stark and grim, no one will question.
Indeed the danger for Catholics is to grow so habituated
to this appalling state of things as almost to take it for
granted, and to assume with a shrug of the shoulders that
nothing can be done about it. There is a cure for this fatal
apathy. It has shed light where darkness had abounded. It
has shaken men out of their lethargy, calling forth a zeal
that sped them to the ends of the earth in their eagerness
to make Christ known and loved. It has been called
"God's special gift to the modern world, through which
He means to restore order on earth by establishing it first
in individual souls."

What can this panacea be for which such seemingly
extravagant claims are made? Is this goldmine, this philos-
opher's stone, a reality indeed, or a foolish dream? And
if it does exist, where is it to be found? It is the teaching
given to the world four hundred years ago by St. Ignatius
Loyola, compressed into a volume unpretentious in size,
and entirely devoid of any attempt at style. He called it
"Spiritual Exercises." Pope Leo XIII declared that the
truths contained on its first page alone would, if applied,
solve the social problems of the world.

It is here that we propose to discover the Ignatian
ideals. The saint also wrote the Constitutions of his order,
and several letters of spiritual direction, but these do little
more than complement and amplify what he had already
set forth in his Exercises. The present volume merely
picks and chooses among the treasures in the storehouse,

holds up for you to look at in the clear light one precious
thing at a time, lays it back again in its place and selects
another and yet another, hoping in this way to induce
you to search diligently for yourself by "making" the
Exercises.

When Ignatius wanted to confer a favor on a friend
he would invite him to spend a month in prayerful study
of his book. To one of his benefactors he wrote: "I desire,
as is only just, to make some return for your kindness and
devotion. In this world I know of no other means of
acquitting even a part of what I owe you, than to persuade you to make the Spiritual Exercises for thirty days
under the director whom I shall send you. . . . Not once
or twice, but as many times as is possible do I beg of you
for the service of God our Lord to do this, so that the
divine Master may not one day reproach me for not
having urged you with all my power, seeing that I can
conceive of or imagine nothing better in this life, whether
for a man's own advancement, or the spiritual advantages
he can draw from them for others."

A word is called for at this stage about the author of
the Exercises. Suppose we flash a few pictures on a screen
and examine them together. First, here is a dashing young
Spaniard, astride his mount, fond of display, vain, skilled
in the use of arms, all keyed up for exploits by which to
win the admiration, possibly the hand, of the noble lady
with whom he was infatuated.

In our next picture we have the same man, lying
wounded in bed, nursing a broken leg, chafing impa-
tiently at the enforced inactivity, and calling out for some
story of romance to read and kill time. What he reads
leads on to our third scene. This is Ignatius plunged in

prayer, kneeling in a cave before the image of Jesus crucified, his whole outlook on life radically and permanently transformed. It was here that he wrote his book, here in the solitude of the cave of Manresa. Here he learned the art of right thinking, illuminated by a superabundance of graces. Here four hundred years ago he was taught by God the cure for the ills that beset our world today.

Pope Pius XI declared St. Ignatius "the heavenly patron of all spiritual exercises, and therefore of institutes, sodalities, and bodies of every kind assisting those who are making these exercises." The same Pope writes in the course of an Encyclical on Retreats: "It is recognized that among all the methods of spiritual exercises which very laudably adhere to the principles of sound Catholic asceticism, one has ever held the foremost place, and, adorned with the full and repeated approbation of the Holy See and honored by the praises of men distinguished for spiritual doctrine and sanctity, has borne abundant fruits of holiness for the space of well-nigh four hundred years.

"We mean the method introduced by St. Ignatius Loyola whom We are pleased to call the chief and peculiar master of Spiritual Exercises; whose admirable book ... stood forth conspicuously as a most wise and universal code of laws for the direction of souls in the way of salvation and perfection; as an unexhausted fountain of most excellent and most solid piety; as a most keen stimulus and a well-instructed guide showing the way to secure amendment of morals and attain the summit of the spiritual life. . . ."

Pope Pius XII was not less emphatic. "In the first

place," he wrote, "it pleases Us to express the highest commendation of the ascetical discipline of St. Ignatius. ... How many men indeed who, because of their absorption in the affairs of this world, were neglecting the things of heaven or were wallowing in the mire of sin, have at last on entering a spiritual retreat lifted their thoughts from the things of earth to those of heaven ... have set their consciences in order, obtained the pardon they craved for their sins, and with it the grace of God and heavenly peace. ... Wherefore, let the members of the family of Ignatius hold this method of retreat most dear. ... Let them strive in season and out of season to have as many people as possible frequent these houses of retreat."

It is probably quite true that "in our anxiety to meet and refute the errors of today, we minimize the power of a simple affirmation of our fundamental Christian synthesis." St. Ignatius' book is just such a complete synthesis. What measure of success it has achieved in lifting men's hearts and minds to God and establishing them in lives of solid piety may be gleaned from the words of the Sovereign Pontiff. It is these words which embolden us to make for the book and its author the claim that here is sure healing for a wounded world; here is light to guide our feet unerringly into the paths of true wisdom.

II

GENERAL DIRECTIONS

MANY Catholic writers have deplored the tendency to isolate religion from life. The rift, they declare, is largely explained by a general ignorance of religion on the part of the educated laity. The formal religious education in many of our secondary schools has been pathetically inadequate. The raw undergraduate with this superficial knowledge of religion often enters a university whose curriculum lacks any real religious orientation. If he is fortunate enough to avoid the pitfalls of cynicism, the barrenness of anticlericalism, and the tragedy of religious indifference, he ultimately emerges into a community not fully conscious of his problem or geared to deal with his special needs.

How would Ignatius tackle the problem raised by this type of Catholic? It is beyond doubt that he would move heaven and earth to induce him to make the Exercises, and if possible for an entire month. That was what he did with Xavier, the gay student of the University of Paris, and all the world knows the transformation effected. This he did for a young man he encountered at Coimbra.

"Did they show you monsters and devils?" this man was asked afterwards.

"Far worse than that; they showed me myself."

You will be disappointed if you merely procure a copy

of the "Spiritual Exercises" and think that by settling down to read it with close attention it will yield its secrets. A first reading, and possibly several repeated readings, may leave you cold. The book, you decide, is jejune and piecemeal. You are not impressed and you wonder vaguely why it has impressed so many before you. "The book," writes Archbishop Goodier, "has been written, not that it may be read, but, that at every step it might be set aside and put into practice. It has been written with the understanding that he who uses it has by his side an interpreter to explain it to him."

The role of this interpreter is important but secondary. He is to propose for meditation a portion of the book to his "exercitant," the person "making" the Exercises, but his exposition is to be brief. His business is merely to "prepare and dispose the soul," and he should "allow the Creator to work immediately with the creature, and the creature with its Creator and Lord." Hence he is not to "preach" the retreat, and there can be little doubt that the lengthy disquisitions which have become almost the accepted usage would meet with the saint's unqualified disapproval.

Ignatius wants no passive listener. An exercitant must exercise himself. It is by no means enough to look in a mirror and discover what he is like and then turn away and "presently forget what manner of man he is." The most important part of the retreat is the period during which, alone with God, the exercitant ponders over in his heart like Mary what he has seen and heard in the lectures. The saint knew well what such prayerful thinking had accomplished in his own case. The ideals for which he had lived hitherto collapsed indeed, but their fall spelled not failure but triumph, not the ending of ambition but the birth of it, elevated, supernaturalized, a new fire leaping up in the heart and consuming worldly dreams of worldly glory. The wounded soldier might have thought life no longer held for him much that was worthwhile. He was to learn, and teach to others, that apparent frustration is often the prelude to real achievement.

The passive listener will come out of the retreat in most cases just confirmed in an existence of useless complacency. Ignatius wants him to taste and feel and lay hold of the soul-shaking truths proposed in his book. He must come to grips with these, not believing them merely, not giving a mere quiescent assent to them, but letting them sink down so deeply into the texture of his very soul that they become realities, the convictions that form the basis of every rightly constructed spiritual edifice. He demands a "real" assent, not a "notional" one, to quote Newman's distinction, an assent that will prove itself by the transformation, interior and exterior, which through God's grace it will effect in the whole future life of the exercitant.

In the mind of Ignatius the ideal way of using his book is to take it away with you into retirement. He would have you free yourself completely from all other employments. Emancipate yourself. Step right out of your ordinary environment and plunge courageously into solitude. He would have you live a whole month apart with God, sealing your lips and tranquilizing your mind and imagination and setting guard over your eyes and ears. He divides the month into four sections, each occupying roughly a week. Each of these weeks has its own particular objective. Thoughts and affections alien to this, however salutary in themselves, must be excluded, so that, for the time being, the exercitant may be able to give his undivided attention to the matter proper to each week.

Here you are given, Pius XI tells you, "not empty silence but the opportunity to examine those most grave and penetrating questions concerning the origin and destiny of man; whence he comes and whither he is going. . . . Retreats of this kind compel the mind of a man to examine more diligently and intently into all the things that he has thought or said or done. . . . In this spiritual arena the mind becomes accustomed to weigh things maturely and with even balance, the will acquires strength and firmness, the passions are restrained by the rule of counsel. . . . The activities of human life, being in unison with the thought of the mind, are effectively conformed to the standard of reason. Lastly the soul attains here to its native nobility and altitude. . . ."

These happy results depend, of course, on divine grace. But it is reasonable to hope for them if the exercitant "prepares and disposes" himself to receive them. This work of preparation depends largely for its success on the thoroughness and earnestness with which the exercitant sets himself free from every pursuit that would divert him from the Exercises. In order to be in a condition of soul to receive what God wants to give him, he must withdraw into solitude and impose upon himself a faithful observance of silence of lips and of mind. To neglect this, to tone down the saint's clear teaching about this, is to nullify the effect.

This is a point of cardinal importance. Exercitants who

have had experience of retreats where this withdrawal was not complete and not sufficiently insisted upon, and who at other times have kept silence absolutely, are amazed at the difference in results. One has often heard them making the contrast afterwards and declaring that in all future retreats it was going to be complete silence every time.

"From this seclusion," writes St. Ignatius, "three principal advantages follow among many others. The first is that when a person separates himself from friends and acquaintances, and likewise from many not-well-ordered affairs, in order to serve and praise God our Lord, he gains great merit before His divine Majesty.

"The second is that when a person has thus withdrawn himself, as his understanding is not divided on many subjects but all his solicitude is placed on one thing only, namely on the service of his Creator and the profit of his own soul, he enjoys a freer use of his natural powers in seeking diligently what he so much desires.

"The third is that the more our soul finds itself alone and in solitude, the fitter it renders itself to approach and unite itself with its Creator and Lord; and the closer it thus draws near to Him, the more it disposes itself to receive graces and gifts from His divine and supreme goodness."

The more carefully these words are studied the more clear it must become that in the mind of Ignatius it would be a lamentable mistake, calculated to ruin the whole fruit of the retreat, to tone them down and permit or condone without grave reason any laxity in the observance of silence.

If we seem to be laboring the point, it is only because

our conviction is so strong. There are places of retreat where no trouble or expense is spared to secure circumstances conducive to the end proposed, where every means is employed except this one. It must be said that this is nothing but a calamity entirely at variance with the explicit directions of our spiritual guides. Such a retreat passes over the soul just as waves pass over a rock. No real change is effected. The exercitant is "like one who wakes up, rolls over, and falls off asleep again."

Is St. Ignatius' book of the Exercises, and a commentary like this one, of any service to a person who finds it impossible to make a retreat? We venture to suggest that it can do much to help such a soul. Indeed, the saint does not fail to offer help to him or her too. He recognizes that not everyone can set aside a full thirty days for prayer and meditation, that, indeed, there will be many who are so oppressed with different occupations as to find it impossible to get away even for a brief period.

If such is the case, what can one do about it?

There is, first, the general principle that the Exercises should be flexible. The priest who gives them should adapt them to the need and capacity of his exercitant. In the case under consideration this adaptation will allow of the Exercises being spread out, a little to be given each day. The saint would wish that a busy man could manage to free himself for an hour or for a half-hour, or even for less if even less is all he can spare. He should be carefully instructed in the meditations of the first week and, in solitude and silence,—as much of it as is compatible with his duties and state of life,—he should apply his faculties to prayerful and serious reflections on the subject matter proposed.

The director must judge whether to give such a person the whole of the Exercises in this way—piecemeal—or whether to confine him to the first week. Generally, the saint thinks, such a person would probably not be the type who would want to go further than the fundamental meditations. If, on the other hand, the director considers that the exercitant is capable of the greater fervor and generosity demanded for the second and subsequent weeks, let him not hesitate to lead him on further.

All this is indicative of another principle often stressed by the saint—get the best results possible. If you cannot secure a hundred per cent, but only eighty, then strive for eighty; if you see that anything more than fifty or forty is not to be attained, then work and leave nothing undone to have at least that much. So, here, if the exercitant cannot give the time all at once, let us break it up in lesser periods; if he cannot rise to the heights of great holiness, let us at least make sure that he repents of his sins, makes a good Confession and resolves to take his eternal salvation seriously henceforth.

Another question that might be asked is: Is the book of Exercises and a commentary such as this any use after the exercitants have made a retreat and returned home? The answer is that such persons should find St. Ignatius' book or this commentary a most useful reminder of the thoughts they pondered and the affections they made and the impulses of divine grace which they experienced. So it cannot but help to take home from the retreat a book which should help to recapitulate the "talks."

As we have pointed out already, there is much more in these meditations than can possibly be absorbed and assimilated in a single meditation. St. Ignatius wants several repetitions, convinced that only by repetition after repetition would these strong convictions be formed which shape the soul to sanctity. Often in the actual retreat there is not much time for such repetitions; hence the value of a written summary, which this little book strives to be. It is thus, in some measure, a substitute for the repetitions.

This book, of course, can also be used as an ordinary "meditation book." For instance, sodalists of our blessed Lady, who have a rule enjoining on them a quarter of an hour's mental prayer every day, should find it helpful.

III

FOUNDATIONS

THERE was the ring of conviction in the letter. "I had the good fortune," it reads, "to make the Exercises for the first time as a student in France in 1951, and since then I have been haunted with the idea of making them better known. . . . I count my first retreat as the biggest grace of my life. The silence and effort at personal reflection demanded by St. Ignatius, and the prayer that results, are a spiritual tonic. . . ."

Father Abram Ryan echoes the teaching of the saint when he writes:

> "I walked down the valley of silence, down the dim voiceless valley, alone,
> And I heard not a sound nor a footstep save only God's and my own."

This is that state of serenity in which the soul is in ideal conditions to speak to God and, what is even more important, to hear Him. Day after day you enter like Moses into the cloud, privileged like him to have private audience with God. Here you assimilate in quite a new way divine truth. If you set out to make this intimate contact with God "with a large heart," the saint is convinced God cannot fail to communicate Himself to you. Within the cloud there is an abundance of divine light and grace.

What material for thought and prayer does Ignatius supply before he bids you enter for the first time into that sanctuary and kneel down in that Presence enveloped in light? "The message which we have heard from him, and announce to you is this: that God is light, and in him is no darkness." [1]

A simple parable may help to illustrate the proposed subject matter for the opening conversation between God and you as you gird yourself for the first session of this audience.

Let me ask you, then, if you can remember the first time you ever saw a watch. It is not likely that you can. Perhaps your father drew it forth from his pocket, dangled the gold chain before your eyes, and directed you to examine the shiny thing hanging at the end.

Your first question? "Daddy, what is it?"

And Daddy, who at that time was for you a living encyclopedia, told you the thing was a watch.

After a moment or two of childish wonder comes your second question: "A watch, Daddy? And what is a watch for?"

Again the oracle spoke and explained that a watch was an instrument for telling the time. Daddy pointed to the hands, called your attention to the fact that they were moving each at a different pace, and that from their position he could know the hour and the minute.

Your third question: "And how does the watch work, Daddy?"

So he opened the cover and showed you the intricate

---

[1] References for Biblical quotations will be found at the end of the book on pp. 178-179.

little wheels and springs, all combining each with the rest
to secure that the watch would fulfil its function as perfectly as possible. You learned that every tiny piece was
important and necessary. If one of these was injured the
watch ceased to tell the time, or at best could no longer
be relied upon to indicate it with accuracy.

What is it? What is it for? How does it work?

When St. Ignatius sends you in for your first private
audience with your heavenly Father, he bids you discuss
with Him three similar questions. What am I? What am I
for? How am I to do it? Basic questions, surely. It is
precisely because the world has forgotten the answers
that it is at this moment being shaken to its foundations.

What am I? I am first of all a creature of God. Salesmen
will exhibit hats and dresses in the manner best calculated
to attract a buyer, and they will label their goods "a new
creation." Creation means something new, something
existing now which had no existence a while ago. How
does it come into existence? Because God called it forth
from nothingness. The weird-shaped hat in the shop window can be called a "creation" only in a very loose and
inaccurate sense, for in this case the "creator" merely
took material already existing and shaped it to his purpose.

My Creator did nothing of this sort. Twenty years ago,
forty, or seventy, I had no being. No one knew me except
Him. From eternity He knows, and plans that at a given
moment He will draw me forth from nothingness, infusing into my body that principle of life which is my soul,
and which I possess at this moment because God by a
special act of His will created it. In the creation of this
soul of mine my parents had no share at all. It came

through the exclusive act of God alone. There are those who think He could delegate to another the power to create thus. But this at least is certain, that in point of fact He never has done so. To our human thinking it might almost seem as if He guarded this marvelous power with jealousy.

Nor is this all. Having created me, my God must now continue to preserve me in His creation. Each beat of my heart is like another creation. I once saw a man on board ship holding his little son aged three over the side to enable him to feed the birds that were following us. If he had let go, the child at that instant would have fallen overboard. But if my heavenly Father "let go," if for a single second He ceased to remember and sustain me in creation, I must immediately lapse not merely to the ground, but back into the nothingness from which He had called me forth in the beginning.

What am I? A creature of God indeed, but much more. I am also a son of God. When I was baptized, I was "born again." My Father adopted me into His family but did for me immeasurably more than any human parents could do for a child they adopt. Human parents can treat the adopted child "as if" he were their own flesh and blood. But he is not, and no amount of affection lavished on him can ever make him a sharer in their life. This is what my heavenly Father does. By Baptism I share in His divine life and became a "real" child of God. "As many as received him he gave the power of becoming sons of God." [2] "Behold what manner of love the Father has bestowed upon us, that we should be called children of God; and such we are." [3]

This divine sonship gives me a claim to a divine inheritance—"if we are sons, we are heirs also." [4] What inheritance is this which is coming to me? "Eye has not seen, nor
ear heard, nor has it entered into the heart of man what
things God has prepared for those who love him." [5]

And what am I for? My dependence on my Creator
and Father is so absolute and complete that words are
altogether inadequate to give me even an inkling of its
true nature. Surely that much is clear from the answers
to my first question. God owns me; I am His property
by every kind of right and title. He owns me because He
freely called me into being. He owns me because on Him
I depend for every movement of my hand or foot, for
every thought passing through my mind, for every word
and for the intelligence to utter it, or to understand what
is said when another addresses me.

His ownership of me He will exercise further when He
summons me out of this world at death. His order is
imperative. Another summons I might disobey or forget.
When He calls I drop at that instant whatever else I may
be doing, how important soever it may seem. He owns
me and to Him at death I give instant and unhesitating
obedience.

What then am I for? As His creature my task is to
render to Him the homage of my will by doing whatever
He wants me to do. As His son I am here to pour out on
my heavenly Father all the love my heart is capable of
giving. What is the watch for? To tell the time. What
am I for? To obey and to love and later to enter upon my
inheritance as a son of God. What am I for? "To praise,
reverence, and serve God," answers Ignatius, "and by

this means to save my soul." There is logic here for the mind. There is also even at this initial stage entrancing music for the heart, the first notes in the hymn of love which, as the Exercises proceed, will climax in a mighty paean.

IV

EXCUSE ME, GOD

GOD'S people were in bondage. He decided to set them free. He chose Moses to be His instrument, but Moses did not want to shoulder the responsibility. "Who am *I*," he demanded, "that I should go to Pharaoh and lead the Israelites out of Egypt? . . . They will not believe me nor listen to my plea. . . . If you please, Lord, I have never been eloquent . . . I am slow of speech and tongue." [1] Perhaps God would look for someone else and let Moses off. But God had made an irrevocable choice.

Elias by God's command had spoken of fearful threats against the people for their sins and had worked miracles in order to add force to his words. But Achab, a wicked king, swore to take the life of the prophet and Elias fled in terror into the desert. Quite spent and weary he flung himself on the ground, buried his head in the sand, and declared to the Lord he could do no more. All he now wanted was to die; there where he lay to give up his soul.

Once more God was insistent, provided the exhausted man with food, warned him that there was still a long life ahead of him and much more work to do.

God ordered Jonas to go to Ninive and preach to the Ninivites, "for the wickedness thereof is come up before me." [2] Jonas was not enthusiastic; indeed he was appalled by the suggestion. He had heard all about the pagan revelries of the place and he was convinced that he was not the right man to tackle them. So down he scurried to the seacoast, boarded a ship that was going to Tharsis, due west, when God had said due east! The rest of the delightful story you must read for yourself, even if you know it already.

The Sacred Heart appeared to St. Margaret Mary and told her He had chosen her to spread this devotion all over the world. The prospect terrified her and she implored Him to ask someone else.

The Curé of Ars ran away from his parish, exactly at the height of his fame as a preacher and confessor, just when his indefatigable labors for souls were bringing forth most fruit. Under cover of darkness he tiptoed out early one morning, and all unobserved took the highway to a monastery. Here he promised himself he could live in peaceful contemplation far removed from those importunate crowds who were eating up every moment of his day and most of his nights too. But the crowds, suspecting where he was, set out after him in hot haste, caught up with him, clapped hands on his shoulders and marched him back to Ars in triumph.

You remember the parable? Lord, I have bought a yoke of oxen, and frankly they interest me much more than the supper You have prepared, so please do not be offended if I do not turn up. Lord, You are asking at a most awkward moment when I am actually on my way to inspect a new farm. Is it really so important that I should be at Your table after all? Lord, I am a newlywed; what a pity to have to disappoint You. But You will understand, I feel sure, and hold me excused.

Each of these incidents is cited in proof of the fact that

even good people can offer resistance to God's will—and do. Our Lord summed up His life by telling us that He came down from heaven not to do His own will but the will of Him that sent Him. Our Lady presented herself in God's sight with the words: "Behold the handmaid of the Lord; be it done to me according to thy word!" [3] The difficulty in accepting St. Ignatius' fundamental principle and living by it is not that it has ever been found to fail. The trouble lies rather in the reluctance of the will, which tends to be satisfied or tries to be satisfied with a lesser good than God.

"A measured contempt for the passing baubles of this world," writes Mr. Christopher Hollis, "is a mark not of sanctity but of common sense." The saints excel in this common sense precisely because they see so clearly that all fears, all doubts, all personal schemes and tastes must be tested on the anvil of the divine will. Like Saul on the Damascus Road the decisive question for them is: "Lord, what wilt thou have me do?" [4]

How does this work out in practice? My heavenly Father has given me His Commandments which He has set like ten great arc-lights along the route that leads home. He has given me the safe guidance of His Church, a source of truth to be dispensed under the unerring direction of His Holy Spirit. He has stored for me as in a reservoir infinite in capacity all the merits acquired by His life and Passion, and He permits me, invites me, presses me urgently to draw freely from this fountain-head for the strength I need to live as He wants me to live and do what He wants me to do.

The will of God I find further in the duties of my state in life. As a married man or woman, as a single person,

as a doctor or nurse, a policeman, a priest, a messenger boy, a farmer, or a university professor, I have certain duties and certain principles to live by. My day's work with all the demands it makes for its conscientious discharge furnishes me with yet another directive in my task of doing His will.

Then there are the circumstances in my life which God permits or ordains—often I cannot see why. There is sickness and unemployment, a bad season, a failure in an examination; there are pleasant things, friendship, holidays, kindness shown to me. "For those who love God all things work together unto good." [5] All these correspond to the works at the back of the watch. He best knows how to produce harmony out of what often seems discord, order out of apparent chaos. "All things shall be well, and all things shall be well, and thou shalt see it thyself that all manner of things shall be well."

The saints are those who permit God to arrange their lives His way. Not only do they try never to oppose His action, but they seek positively to cooperate with it fully. Holman Hunt painted his picture "The Light of the World." It shows our Lord with lighted lantern in His right hand knocking with His left on the door of the soul. Somebody remarked that the artist had forgotten to paint the handle on the outside. "No," he replied, "I have not forgotten. There is a handle, but it is on the inside of the door."

V

USE OF CREATURES

THERE is something very pathetic in the spectacle of our God deigning to ask, to invite, to urge, to argue with us, seeming as if He refuses to take no for an answer. The handle is on the inside; why do we refuse to turn it and fling the door wide open? Because of the tyranny of what St. Ignatius would call "creatures." What does he mean?

The term in the mind of the saint embraces all the circumstances of my life such as mental ability or the lack of it, the climate in which I live, the peculiarities of my neighbor, the friends I have made, the things that annoy, the things that please me, what I naturally like and what I naturally dislike. The term penetrates into my inward dispositions so as to include virtues like justice and charity, faults of character like impatience or jealousy. So comprehensive is it that it may be said to contain everything that affects my life how remotely soever except God and my soul.

Now when I consider these creatures I find that they readily enough divide themselves into two classes. There are those which naturally I like such as the pleasant sunshine or the companionship of a true friend; and there are those which I quite definitely shrink from such as disease, loneliness, physical or mental pain. Nature's instinctive reaction is to seek the creature I like and shirk the creature I dislike. In contemplating Ignatian ideals it is of the first importance to recognize that this standard of choice is unsound.

If an artist paints a picture, he selects and uses the brushes and paints just insofar as they help to produce the result he wants. If a surgeon performs an operation he will employ the instruments which he considers most suitable to his patient in these precise circumstances. It is easy to imagine what would happen if surgeon or artist allowed himself to be ruled by caprice, merely by what he found most pleasant to use.

Man is made only for love, to prove his love of God by praise, reverence, and service. Hence he should question every creature that presents itself to him: "How much divine love can I extract from you?" Just as the bee collecting honey has an "interest" in each flower only insofar as each flower provides honey, so man, if he finds a creature from which he can extract no love of God at all —as in the case of sin—instantly passes by that creature. He employs the creature insofar and only insofar as it helps to an increase of divine love in his soul.

Hence the role of creatures is one of servitude. In the measure in which they are permitted to govern my choices irrespective of the end in view, they become tyrants. This is what we saw happening in varying degrees in some of the incidents quoted in our previous chapter.

It is beyond question that creatures which are naturally pleasant can be made to help the soul Godwards. He it is who has made them thus, and they can often be like the drop of oil in the machine, ensuring that it run smoothly. For all that, it seems clear that His best friends tend to be chary and fearful of self-deception here. They invariably incline toward retrenching such creatures rather than toward multiplying them. They practice consistently "the art of doing without," and this not only in material things, but even more in surrender, often unsuspected, of their interior preferences and opinions. This is their life-long struggle for mastery over creatures. They call it detachment or independence of one's natural likes and dislikes. St. Ignatius' word for it is "indifference." It sets the soul free from the tyranny of creatures.

"Every one of you who does not renounce all that he possesses, cannot be my disciple." [1] There is no loophole here for one who would compromise. It little matters, St. John of the Cross writes, whether a bird is tied with a silken string or a strong cord. In neither case can it soar into the freedom and delight of sunshine and sky. "One single unmortified passion," says the Jesuit Père Rigoleu, "one habit which we have neglected to correct, one attachment with which we are unwilling to part, may retain a soul for whole years, yea for an entire lifetime, lingering on the threshold of the most perfect state, union with God, into which He would have introduced it had this particular impediment been removed."

We know now why in the very title of his book St. Ignatius warned us about "self-conquest." He wrote the Exercises to help us put order in our lives, to teach us how to overcome "inordinate affections," and thus arrive at a right decision regarding any problem, especially the problem of vocation in life. There can be no coming to terms with a self-deception to which he knows us to be so prone. We may never indeed attain to the complete detachment reached by the saints, but he would have us try, and refuse to be beaten.

"God is light and in him is no darkness." [2] As the soul once more prepares to go into the Presence it may expect the penetrating light to reveal to it the roots of its own inordinate attachments. They will be rather ugly to look at, but let not the soul be discouraged. No man is happy unless he bends his back to the task of digging out those roots. It is hard work, but infinitely worthwhile. "If every year we rooted out one fault we would soon become perfect men."

The doctrine of the saints about detachment, sound as it is in itself, still calls for a word of warning as it is to be applied to each individual soul. One has known instances where too violent and sudden a change has resulted in ultimate spiritual shipwreck, where too much rigidity in periods of training produced in later years a reaction that despised all practice of detachment, and sought by constant self-indulgence compensation for what had been too forcefully withdrawn.

In all such cases it is not the principle that is wrong so much as the unwise and incorrect application of it. A beginner in the spiritual life can subject himself to restraint in a spirit of stoic indifference which is devoid of love. But the detachment of the saints is a growth which stems from a contempt of creatures and what they can offer, except where they offer to lead the soul nearer to God. It is easy to despise the creature when one has become inflamed with love of the Creator. Detachment from one leads to closer attachment to the other.

To pilot a soul successfully between the Scylla of over-leniency and the Charybdis of overregimentation often calls for consummate skill on the part of the soul's spiritual guide.

VI

SELF-KNOWLEDGE

ST. Ignatius' broken leg had been badly reset. He would be lame in future. Rather than endure this humiliation he ordered the leg to be broken again and set again. At the time he probably considered this to be courage; later in the clearer light of grace he recognized it as pride.

There is a fund of secret pride deep in the heart. Those who come closest to the divine light in intimacy with God discern it. The discovery produces in them a chastening humility, a true knowledge of self, the only secure rock on which to raise the edifice of holiness. "It may be said," wrote the Spanish Jesuit, Father Alvarez de Paz, "that there are two omnipotent beings, God and a truly humble soul. God is omnipotent to give, and a humble soul is omnipotent to receive."

Hence the next step for the exercitant is to sift thoroughly the motives which impel him to act. Where he finds these to be imperfect the saint would have him purify them, supplanting them little by little by motives which are supernatural. The Ignatian ideal in this regard is admirably proposed by the saint in an instruction to his sons. "Let all endeavor," he writes, "to have a right intention not only in their state of life, but also *in all particulars*. In these they must sincerely seek how they may best serve and please the divine goodness for His own sake. . . . *In all things* let them seek God, casting off as much as they can all love of creatures and fixing their whole heart on the Creator alone. They must love Him in all creatures; they must love all creatures in Him. This is what His most holy and divine will desires from them."

You sometimes hear that we are in this world to save our souls. Certainly we are. But Ignatius has not set that object, however praiseworthy, in the first place. What we are here for primarily is to praise God, reverence God, serve God. Our eternal salvation will follow on this, but with Ignatius that seems to be almost an afterthought. The reason is that he is preoccupied with God. With him God's glory is paramount; beside it nothing else is worth a moment's consideration. Whether it is a question of hammering a nail in the wall or opening a new mission in a distant land, the motive with him is identical. "In *all* things let them seek God. . . ." "For the greater glory of God" has become the motto of his Order. The phrase occurs nearly three hundred times in his Constitutions— once, almost, on each page.

This has been set down by way of answering a charge sometimes brought against him. It is said that his doctrine concentrates too much on self, and it is claimed that the soul would advance in holiness more swiftly and more surely by fixing its gaze upon its God, upon Christ, and by means of this "positive approach" under the action of grace rid itself of its faults and purify its motives the more speedily.

Assuredly, as we shall see, the saint was not ignorant of the advantage of the "positive approach." But in this first week of his Exercises he is dealing with a novice who is moving in a new world, a recruit who at this initial stage must be taught how to "prepare and dispose" himself for the divine action.

Further he is envisaging for the most part men who after completing the Exercises will find their vocation in "the world." Plunged into the many distractions of a busy life these need, generally speaking, a more systematized spirituality than is required by a cloistered monk. So he suggests certain devices by which they can help themselves, and one of these is the Particular Examen of Conscience.

And just as the soul's salvation seemed to him to come in logical order only after the glorifying of God, so now the soul's perfection is recognized as desirable, not at all for the soul's own comfort, not that it may, so to say, smooth its feathers and dwell complacently on its achievement, but only because the more perfect a soul is, the more will it glorify God. Hence it is Godward direction all the time.

The soul must not be dismayed if under the penetrating rays of the strong light of grace it discovers in itself imperfections and imperfect motives, the existence of which were until now not even suspected. The discovery itself already marks considerable advance. St. Francis de Sales advises such a soul: "Note that those who have the greatest number of bad inclinations are those who can reach a greater perfection. Do not be at all discouraged to find in yourself such bad tendencies since by the goodness of God you have a superior will which can overrule all this."

The important thing is to be prompt and persevering in the unexciting task of purifying the soul. Let us put

some order into the process, counsels Ignatius. Do not
begin by scrubbing the floor and then sweeping dust from
the walls and ceiling. Take in hand first the fault that is
most glaring, the one possibly which is the root of many
others—your predominant fault, if you can discover what
it is. Watch it particularly. When you rise in the morning
resolve quietly to keep a vigilant eye on it, and examine
yourself twice each day on how you have succeeded.
You could perhaps keep a short record in writing by
which from time to time to check your progress. If there
is a failure, it would be excellent to impose on yourself
a penance. (I knew an old man who would refuse to
smoke his pipe as a penance if he ever lost his temper.)

Such importance does Ignatius attach to this "Particular Examen" that he wishes us to use it not only while
we are making the Exercises but throughout the rest of
our lives. He would have us employ it for ridding ourselves of sin and imperfection, concentrating on one fault
at a time and diligently following his instructions in
making war upon it. Similarly, we can specialize by its
means in one virtue at a time, cultivating charity or a
spirit of prayer, exercising ourselves in "humble and
mean offices" which should, he hopes, result in the virtue
of humility.

One of the important functions of the Particular Examen is to teach us how to purify our hearts by discovering the selfish motives from which we act, and lead us
little by little to act "in all things" small or great from
the motive of God's love and God's glory alone. Hence,
says Archbishop Goodier, the work undertaken, "be it
the abstrusest scientific problem or only the washing of
a dish, can never be too perfectly done. Love will make

a man do what nothing else will; love will demand perfection when any other motive will be satisfied with mediocrity."

This white-light purity of motive is the goal set before members of the Apostleship of Prayer. The essential condition for membership is the faithful repetition of the Morning Offering. But the ideal goes much farther. The ideal would have that Offering actualized throughout the entire day following. The ideal demands that as far as possible we live in continuous, constant consciousness of our Offering, so that it affects the doing of each act, sublimating it, supernaturalizing it, cleansing it of all selfish interest or motive, and presenting it thus purified as a prayer, an act of love, to be accepted by the heavenly Father. "For those who love God all things work together unto good." [1]

Thus the Particular Examen can be employed in extirpating sin and imperfection, and not the less effectively in helping the soul to grow in divine love. It is not true to say that it overstresses the human element. But it is, if you wish, a human device, intended to help men whose lives are cast in very human circumstances. Fidelity to such devices insofar as they prove useful to the particular soul is bound to call down an abundance of divine graces, through which alone holiness can be attained. *Facienti quod in se est....* God does not withhold such graces from those who give practical proof of their earnest desire to receive them by "preparing and disposing the soul."

The Master lay fast asleep in Peter's boat. A violent storm swept suddenly down over Genesareth from the surrounding hills. Jesus' friends on board were terrified. They trimmed the sails, put out their oars, and tugged

mightily against the wind, but all to little purpose. Finally
they awakened Him: "Lord, save us, we are perishing." [2]
He opened His eyes, rose up, and, standing there on the
side of the boat, lifted both arms in a commanding gesture. Above the roar of the waves there was heard His
order: "Peace! Be still!" [3] The rough elements yielded
instant obedience. There was a great calm.

The apostles employed their human devices. They gave
evidence of their good will to do whatever was in their
power to do. *Facienti quod in se est. . . .* God helps those
who help themselves—a principle which properly understood is indispensable to him who would discover the
Ignatian ideal and strive to realize it in his own daily
living.

VII

MY SINS

AS the first week of the Exercises advances, St. Ignatius directs me to put myself before God like a prisoner standing in the dock in the presence of his judge. Having seen so far my sublime destiny here and hereafter, he wants me now to examine the reverse side of the medal. The sight of my sins is well calculated to stir up in my heart that sense of "shame and confusion of face," that deep sorrow which may express itself even in bitter tears as often as I recall my black ingratitude to God.

Sin is a burden, a heavy burden, the heaviest load that can ever be placed on your shoulders to carry. Unless a man's conscience through repeated excesses has lost all edge, it will surely inflict a smarting wound the moment the sinful act is completed, perhaps indeed in the very act of sinning. Unless the heart has grown utterly callous the sinner will find it ready to sink down into the depths of despair as often as he thinks of his sin, as often as he remembers that on that day, alone or with those companions or with that companion, during the day or during the night, in his home or place of work, during holidays, during youth or middle age or even when he was quite old, he did those acts which now he recognizes to be degrading to his manhood.

Worse than degrading, they are a fearful insult to

God's infinite holiness. For Ignatius the most frightful evil of sin is not its effect on the sinner, however terrible. Most shocking of all for a man who cared for nothing except the greater glory of God is the fact that sin is an offense against the divine majesty, the thwarting of the plan conceived for man by the God who loves him to excess.

There will probably be times when the sinner will try to laugh airily at the sinful deeds he has done. He will even cast ridicule on persons whose efforts to love and serve God are a reproach to himself. But deep down in the secret places of his soul, unless again he has become quite depraved, there lies a lurking sense of shame and a tasting of bitter remorse for his sin. And this the sinner knows very well.

Even granting that for a time he succeeds in smothering the voice of conscience, it is certain that the effort is a mere drug. Its effects are only temporary. Sooner or later the awakening will come, and the more heavily the conscience has been drugged the more poignant will the disillusionment be.

It is easy then to understand why our Lord, who habitually was meek and humble of heart, who always went more than halfway to meet any sinner who showed signs of true repentance, was yet moved by an anger fearful to see when He came in contact with sinners who persisted in their sins. The strong denunciations which such sinners called forth are indication not only of wrath but of love too. For He sees that sin is ruining His masterpiece. The soul created by God to God's own image and likeness He sees to be trembling on the very brink of eternal doom. At this moment nothing stands between that soul and eternity in hell. Language is inadequate to express the anguish which pierces the heart of Christ at such a spectacle.

Small wonder either that the immaculate soul of Christ drew back in horror and loathing from the vision of sin. Sin it was that filled Him with nausea as He knelt in agony in Gethsemani. This is the place to see sin in its true colors. Kneel here beside Him, counsels Ignatius, and look and learn. He lies flat on His face, His whole body quivering in the greatness of His sorrow and disgust.

Rest your two hands for a moment on those trembling shoulders. A clammy wetness clings to them. Stand up. Come out from under the trees into the full light of the moon and turn up your hands and examine them. Your hands are red, red with the precious blood of the Son of God. Sin did that. Sin forced that blood through the pores of His body. Sin, concerning which your modern gay world talks so glibly; sin, so generously condoned and smiled upon by an intelligentsia grown too big for the Ten Commandments; sin did that. Look at your hands and understand what God thinks of sin.

But never forget that our Lord was sinless and that what He endures in His Passion is borne for the sins of others. If He who is without sin must needs suffer this for others, what then must they expect who are stained with the crime of personal sins, who sin with defiance, who glory in their shameful deeds, finding their satisfaction in prowling in wolfish fashion among the sinless to betray them and slay them? If this be done in the green wood, what shall be done in the dry?

Ignatius would now have me go down on my knees in the sight of my God and listen to the sentence which

might so often have been pronounced upon me for my
sins. Why was it not spoken? Why am I not in hell? It
may well be that there are souls in hell for fewer mortal
sins than I have committed. What is the explanation?
There is one, one only. In the case of these others He
exercised justice; in my case it was mercy, boundless
mercy, wider than the vast expanse of the ocean, for-
giving me even to seventy times seven times.

As a Catholic I believe in the forgiveness of sins. I
believe that no matter what depths of depravity I may
have sounded, a good Confession will lift me out of the
morass. I believe that after this good Confession there is
now no longer any need for anxiety about those sins
of mine, how grievous soever they may have been. I
believe that when I stand before God's judgment seat
the devil dare not utter against me a word of accusation
on the score of these sins. He would instantly be silenced
and told to his confusion that sentence had already been
passed on those sins of mine. It was the complete pardon
that fell from the lips of a merciful Christ in that good
Confession.

My forgiveness is conditioned of course by my disposition. I must be sincerely sorry, I must confess fully,
I must have my mind made up that aided by divine grace
I will shun sin and its occasions in future. If I am prepared
to do my part I believe that though I have been a Judas
or a Magdalene, Jesus at once puts all my crimes behind
His back. Forthwith they are buried in the depths of the
sea. All He now desires is that I forget about them—at
least insofar as the memory of them would cause me
disquiet or distrust in His mercy. But the thought of my

offenses might well serve as a powerful argument for everlasting gratitude, an incentive to a love of Christ which has been accentuated by the very fact that I have proved false, and yet have been so readily and lovingly received back.

St. Thérèse "never refused our Lord anything from the age of three." But still she writes: "It is not because I have been preserved free from mortal sin that I lift up my heart to God in trust and love. I am *certain* that even if I had on my conscience every imaginable crime, I should lose nothing of my confidence, but I would throw myself, my heart broken with sorrow, into the arms of my Savior. . . . I know too well what to believe concerning His mercy and His love."

Despair, doubt, disquiet of mind, shame and confusion of face—all these Ignatius would have me prepared for as I watch, passing me by, the procession of sins which I have committed. But it is very characteristic of him to introduce here into meditations which of their nature are not calculated to console, the note of love. As I contemplate hell, he wants me to pray that if through my faults I should forget the *love* of the eternal Lord, at least the fear of punishment may help me not to fall into sin. "Perfect love casts out fear." [1] But fear there must be until that love has become perfect.

In his *Rules for Thinking with the Church* St. Ignatius again talks about fear and love. "Although it is above all things praiseworthy to serve God out of pure love, yet we ought much to praise the fear of His divine majesty, because not only is filial fear a pious and most holy thing, but even servile fear—when man does not attain to anything better or more useful—is of great help toward rising out of mortal sin and, after he has risen out of it, he easily attains to filial fear, which is wholly acceptable and pleasing to God our Lord, because it is inseparable from divine love."

Hell is always a terrifying possibility, as long as the soul remains imprisoned in the body. There have been those who after many devoted years of service of God gave up the struggle and, it would seem, died unrepentant. Steadying truths like these may not be glossed over, nor the reasonable fear they engender be discredited. So Ignatius, the realist, orders almost peremptorily, that the meditation on hell is never to be omitted.

The way of fear is good; "the fear of the Lord is the beginning of wisdom." [2] But only the beginning. So far Ignatius has merely pushed open the door of his treasure-house and given us a glimpse of the good things inside. That would be a sorry ideal for a man with vision like his which would stop short at the threshold, at avoidance of sin and the resolve to escape hell. That is as much as he can hope for from a certain type of exercitant. But there are others from whom much more can be expected, and to these he now proceeds to point out "a yet more excellent way." [3]

VIII

EXCELSIOR!

BEFORE embarking on the second week we suggest for reasons that will become clear as we go along, that you turn first to the opening chapter of St. John's first epistle.

You know the readiness and conviction with which men speak when relating a personal experience. A person visits America and when he comes home scenes he has witnessed and people he has met remain vividly in his mind. Quite spontaneously he will describe the places and different events and tell you all about the conversations he has had with some of America's remarkable men.

Now St. John had a personal experience which left an indelible mark on his mind and heart and contributed profoundly to the forming of his character. He has lived on terms of intimate contact with Jesus Christ, the Son of God, and he cannot stop speaking about it. He opens his first epistle by telling us that he has *heard* of Christ, more, that he has *seen* Him with his own eyes, that he has *gazed* upon him and *touched* Him with his hands. It seems as if he realizes that the haunting remembrance of such privileges can never again leave him.

He had *heard* about Him. Indeed he could not help hearing, for the whole countryside was stirred with tales of His marvelous deeds and words of authority and power.

John had listened perhaps to the fiery exhortations of his namesake at the Jordan. He had heard of Christ from some of his own familiar friends—from Peter, or Nathaniel, or his brother James.

Having heard *about* Him, John now decides to investigate and make it his business to find Him and listen for himself while Jesus is speaking. On him, as on every rightly disposed soul, the effect is immediate and lasting. "Never has man spoken as this man." [1] It would be interesting to reckon the number of times in his Gospel and Epistles John recounts this experience—"I have heard him speaking." In His language there was simplicity allied to profundity of thought, there was beauty and force, there was authority, there was power, there was pathos, and inexorable logic. The Speaker was uncompromising where principle was at stake but abounding in compassion and sympathy when confronted with a repentant sinner.

Such is the man I have heard, John seems to exclaim. Believe me, this is no mere man. We know and have believed that this is indeed the true Son of God. Neither could you doubt it if like me you had been privileged to listen to the words that fell from His divine lips.

John had *seen* Him too. At first he had looked upon Him with the interest which any remarkable stranger might call forth. "We saw Him with our eyes." But the next word he uses marks a big advance. "We have looked through Him (*Perspeximus*). This implies not merely that he rested his eyes on the Prophet, but that there broke in on his gaze the light to discern who and what He is in some such way as Peter, who exclaimed: "Thou art the Christ, the Son of God who hast come into the world." [2] For this magnificent confession Peter was praised, "for flesh and blood has not revealed this to thee, but my Father in heaven." [3] What a breath-taking experience it must have been for Peter! Divine Grace illuminated his mind and he recognized the divinity of Christ. Such would seem to have been the experience of the venerable Simeon, when he held in his arms the Infant Christ. To him too was granted light to realize that divinity reposed there under his eyes. Similarly on Thabor, where John and Peter and James were granted a fleeting glimpse of the divinity hidden under the veils of the sacred humanity and were intoxicated with joy.

This is no longer merely to behold Christ, merely to look upon Him as you might regard a passing acquaintance. It is to penetrate beneath the surface and to make the overwhelming discovery for oneself that one is literally standing in the Presence of God. Mere "flesh and blood" cannot make this discovery; the awe-struck soul has fallen under God's direct action, and is aware of it.

Not even here, St. John goes on, did my experience end. For I was also permitted to *touch* Him with these hands of mine. It was the privilege everyone sought, because when one touched Him "power went forth from him." [4] Into John too, "the disciple whom Jesus loved," [5] power went forth from the Sacred Heart, to mold him, and enlighten him, to inflame with ardent love, to confirm him in his life of zeal.

Having heard about Him, having listened to Him, having looked upon Him with my own eyes, having been favored with the gift of discernment enabling me to recognize His Godhead utterly holy, having been allowed to rest these hands of mine upon Him, can you wonder that there is now left me only one longing—to gather the whole world together and persuade all that "in him was life, and the life was the light of men," [6] that He is light in whom there is no darkness, and that our stupendous vocation as Christians is to walk in light, set free from the shackles of sin, actually to share in His own divine life?

There is eagerness and insistency in his manner of delivering this message, for he is speaking of what he has seen and heard. There is intense conviction, and words seem to come from him tumbling one over the other in the impetuosity of his longing to share with us the truth he has found. "These things we write to you that you may rejoice and our joy may be full." [7] We are simply bearing witness to what we have seen and heard. We are declaring to you with absolute authority that Christ is God. That is why we are writing to you, for whatever else you miss in life you simply must not fail to come to the knowledge and love of Christ. Whatever else you achieve or fail to achieve is of little importance, provided you follow in His footsteps, share by grace in the new life He has brought into the world, lead as many souls as possible to the inexhaustible source from which the streams of this life emanate—the Heart of the God-Man, Jesus Christ, our Lord.

It would be very easy to trace the same effect in the life of every other man or woman who grows in knowledge of Jesus Christ. There are many who have merely an intellectual knowledge of Him; they know what is written about Him and they give to it the cold assent of the mind, almost the same with which they accept a proposition of Euclid. How the burning heart of John would go out to them in intense compassion, understanding, as he would, the immensity of their loss!

Like John, Ignatius too had heard and seen, and the hearing and the seeing produced in him the same result. In his second week there is that sense of urgency, the goad of divine love, as he constantly bids the exercitant to pray for an "intimate knowledge" of Jesus Christ. This is not knowledge *about* Him—though that will help. Neither is it the knowledge acquired in a school of theology—though that too can be an immense advantage. But this "intimate knowledge" is available to every soul of good will. It is often found in the lives of the "foolish ones" of this world, those who with the simple faith of little children enter, while still on this earth, into the kingdom of heaven.

It is thus an experimental knowledge. The soul knows not only because it has read books or listened to spiritual conferences, that all it has ever learned about Jesus Christ is true. There is realization. The soul understands further that there are still endless avenues to be explored. Even with the knowledge vouchsafed it, it sees itself still standing only on the very fringe of this new country. The knowledge of Christ is inexhaustible; to contain all that could be said or written of Him the world itself would not be large enough.

To help the soul toward this "intimate knowledge," in the measure destined for it by divine grace, is the great objective of the saint in the second and subsequent weeks. "Intimate" or "interior" knowledge, the gift of grace by which the soul knows from personal experience the truth that is Christ, the love and lovableness that is Christ—such knowledge is a burning brand starting up in the heart an all-consuming fire of love. Impossible to conceive one

without the other. And if that love is the genuine article
it will be active. "When God once takes possession of a
heart, He does not long remain inactive." The charity of
Christ translates itself swiftly into the deeds of love. Like
John, like Peter, like Paul, like Ignatius, the soul feels a
holy constraint to tell the world, to persuade the world
that is steeped in darkness that it has discovered the true
light.

And in all this the soul is imitating Christ who came to
cast fire on the earth and vehemently desired to see it
enkindled. Intimate knowledge, burning love, close dis-
cipleship—these are "the better gifts" proposed to the
soul as Ignatius advances to meet it and invite it to enter
"with a large heart" into the second week of his Spiritual
Exercises. The saint has experienced what has been finely
described as "the invasion of divine grace into his soul."
He would have the whole world share his secret.

IX

WE'RE INVINCIBLE

IF you are unexpectedly brought before a beautiful
picture your first reaction is a general impression of
admiration for this work of genius. It takes time to catch
your breath and examine each detail at your leisure. After
your first sweeping survey of the masterpiece you want
to sit down in front of it and allow it to "grow" on you
by degrees.

St. Ignatius, enamored of the God-Man, speaks of Him
from now on out of the abundance of his heart. He knows
exactly what it is that he ardently desires his exercitant to
discover, "Christ's love which surpasses knowledge." [1]
He is well aware that if a director be qualified to prepare
and dispose the soul of the exercitant at this point, and if
for his own part the exercitant gives full cooperation,
gigantic results may be confidently expected. God does
not give the spirit by measure. The task here is fraught
with such possibilities for the soul that one seems to detect
a sense of tension in the saint's instructions and meditations as he takes his disciple aside and introduces him into
this second week.

The exercitant must first get a general idea of the stature
of Christ and His mission. He is invited to spend one
entire day prayerfully contemplating Christ as King who
came into this world to overthrow the kingdom of Satan

47

and establish the kingdom of His Church. "Fix your eyes steadily upon Him," Ignatius would say. "Watch Him intently as He travels up and down the length and breadth of Palestine, now talking to the fishermen at the shore, now seated on the slope of a hill preaching to the multitudes gathered around Him at His feet, now giving His undivided attention to the needs of some individual person—Nicodemus, or the woman of Samaria, the blind man of Jericho, the leper begging a cure, the widow of Naim."

Wherever you find Him there is always one interest dominant in His words and actions. He is intent on spreading His "kingdom"—though it is only by slow degrees that He unfolds His plan fully. "My will is to conquer the whole world, and all My enemies, and thus to enter into the glory of My Father." This means the overthrowing of sin, and with a word of command He drives Satan out of the souls of men. This means vigorous action where principle is at stake, and this fearless man turns the money tables topsy-turvy in the temple, seizes a whip and drives buyers and sellers in headlong confusion out of His Father's house. In challenging tones He demands an explanation why they dared to change this house of prayer into a den of traffic. The spreading of the kingdom means calling sin by its right name, and never does He hesitate to tear ruthlessly from the smug faces of hypocrites the mask that hides their vice.

Catholicism is a terrific struggle with the forces of evil to bring about the revolution, world revolution, which is the spreading of the kingdom of Christ. Compromise is impossible. "He who is not with me is against me, and he who does not gather with me, scatters." [2]

The King sends out a clarion call for volunteers to join

up and with Him win the world back to God. "You and I will toil together," He says. "The task in hand is the most divine of all divine works, the salvation of souls. There will be plenty to suffer, but we will encourage and sustain each other by our mutual example. I am not going to ask you to do anything on this campaign which I have not done myself. Then, when victory comes, you will surely share in the rich reward of those who have served loyally."

When victory comes, you will observe; not *if*. That is a point of capital importance, never to lose sight of. We're invincible and we know it. We know it first of all because our divine Leader has given us the assurance that the gates of hell will never prevail. He has warned us that there will be wars and rumors of war; He has said we must expect to be hated by all men for His sake; He foretold that there would be scandals, that some would prove to be traitors; He did not conceal the future persecutions in store, nor did He minimize the fury and satanic energy with which they would rage against His Church.

All this is what He told us to expect. Our expectations have been fulfilled. They are being fulfilled today. "You shall weep and lament but the world shall rejoice; and you shall be sorrowful but your sorrow shall be turned into joy. A woman about to give birth has sorrow because her hour is come. But when she has brought forth the child, she no longer remembers the anguish, for her joy that a man is born into the world. And you therefore have sorrow now; but I will see you again and your heart shall rejoice, and your joy no one shall take from you.... Take courage, I have overcome the world." [3]

Persecution, dungeon, fire and sword, concentration

camp, mock trials—all that sort of thing the Catholic Church takes for granted. It is her history for two thousand years. But with the same serenity and insistence comes the repeated assurance that we are invincible.

There is also the testimony of history, substantiating statement. For all these centuries the Catholic Church has faced hatred and opposition. It would be a congenial task to reckon how often her enemies announced to the world that she was in her death struggle, and not less interesting to count the number of times she renewed her youth. Her very history is proof of her divinity. Even the scandals occurring in the ranks of her own children, so zealously exploited by men who hate her, even these contribute their testimony to a principle within her of divine life that refuses to die. No merely human institution could possibly have survived a fraction of the persecution that has been her lot from the beginning.

At school a boy will be proud to be elected captain, to get a place on the college team. On leaving school he will work to reach the top of his profession. A girl will become a nurse, an air hostess, a lawyer or doctor; she will hope Prince Charming may come along and beg her to marry him. Different ambitions rise up in different hearts. In many cases to realize them is to write your name on sand. But to hear the appeal of the King, to ponder prayerfully on what it implies—the privilege of it, the responsibility it entails—and then to reach out with both hands to accept it because your heart is ablaze with love of Jesus Christ, this is to inscribe your name on the immortal Roll of Honor.

The going is likely to be hard. If the communists get you they may dump you into a concentration camp and entertain themselves by torturing you into making "confessions" of crimes that never so much as entered into your mind. You may easily enough be called upon to shed your blood for the King, even to die for Him. You will surely be asked to live for the King and there are times when that is the harder thing to do. But hardship there is going to be for sure. Many of His volunteers, when by chance they found themselves with nothing to suffer for Him, had no peace of mind till suffering came back again into their lives. They were haunted all the while, you see, by the thought that the King Himself had had so much hardship, and they felt a sense of shame and inadequacy, as if He somehow was forgetting them if they too did not have to suffer with Him and like Him.

"Hath He diadem as monarch that His brow adorns?
Yes, a crown in very surety—but of thorns.
If I find Him, if I follow, what His guerdon here?
Many a sorrow, many a labor, many a tear."

A young priest volunteered for mission work in Alaska —the most difficult mission in the Church. "I wanted to be in a place," he explained, "where whatever I would do for souls would be known to nobody except Him alone, and where I would suffer much and would have nobody except Him with whom to share my suffering."

The King appeals to your reason, showing you that the proposed campaign is worthwhile. But "if you rely upon reason more than upon the virtue that subjects to Jesus Christ, you will seldom, or never, become an enlightened man. For God will have us wholly subject to Him, and transcend all reason by an inflamed love." Ignatius, too,

4·14·24

expects you to love greatly. In Christ's army there are volunteers only, no conscripts, because love is the motive. When he has guided you through his Exercises he wants to speed you out into a famishing world that has grown cold and cynical because it has forgotten how to love. "I have come," says the King, "to cast fire upon the earth, and what will I but that it be kindled?" [4]

The Person who calls, the work to be done, the methods to be employed, all three combine to show how justified Ignatius is in demanding excellence. "As mediocrity is not the spirit of the Church it certainly is not the spirit of Ignatius or Ignatianism. Though he is understanding and tolerant of weakness, Ignatius places no limits to his quest for perfection. The best and the finest available means are to be used in the most complete service of the highest good. Wherever it was conceivably feasible he would tolerate nothing second-rate in the training of his men, nor anything second-rate in what they needed for their purposes. They were to search for the most solid and the most comprehensive exposition of the Christian Faith and way of life according to the needs of the times. . . . In other words, Ignatius strove in every fashion to assist the Church to make the fullest impact upon the thought and upon the imagination of his time. . . .

"We need men of great rectitude, spiritual and mental, who see first things first, and lesser things in relation to those that are first and last. We need, secondly, men of humble, total dedication."

X

IGNATIAN PRAYER

IGNATIUS has been described as a Carthusian let loose. It is certain that the Carthusian Order attracted him from the very beginning of his conversion. He seriously contemplated joining it and made careful inquiries about the details of the Rule observed at Burgos. His own austerities at the time rivaled those of any monastery. His longing for seclusion led him to the retirement of Manresa where he was favored with gifts in prayer of the highest mystical order. His autobiography—the few pages which escaped when he destroyed the rest—abounds in accounts of visions in which he is brought face to face with our Lord or our Lady or the saints.

Such experiences are entirely gratuitous and Ignatius is well aware that they are no proof of the sanctity of the person who receives them. He was one of the few who refused to believe in Maddalena della Croce, a Dominican nun reputed far and wide to be a saint, recipient of marvelous mystical graces, and who in the end was discovered to be a fraud. Christopher Hollis writes that he would not give credence to the claims of Ignatius himself to visions and locutions, were it not that the Church has canonized him, and that only direct supernatural aid can account for his achievements. Merely that the saint was a shrewd man of excellent judgment weighs little or not at all. There

53

are blind spots of illusion "which one surprisingly discovers in men otherwise most normal."

It used to be the fashion to talk about "The Ignatian
Method of Prayer." Commentators on the Exercises were
of the opinion that the saint wanted to dragoon people
into prayer, and in the effort to do so to drill them by
means of a series of "Exercises" much like a top sergeant
with a squad of raw recruits on the barrack square! No
room was to be left for individuality; little even, it would
seem, for the action of the Holy Spirit on the soul. Here
was a well-tried system by which to approach God. It
was *the* way taught in the school of Ignatius. If, like the
boy David struggling under the weight of the heavy armor, you found it unwieldy, then was your spirituality
suspect, and well-intentioned directors would raise re-
proving fingers to warn you against deceit and illusion.

There is no one-track way to God in prayer and it is
quite certain that if any man was thoroughly aware of this
fact, the man was Ignatius Loyola. "It is a thing full of
danger," he writes, "to wish to force everyone to God by
the same path . . . the person who does this shows how
ignorant he is of the variety of the gifts of God's Holy
Spirit." Given his own experiences in prayer, this is just
the sort of thing we should expect him to say. In the Exercises, it is true, he plans the ground with minute care;
in a matter so important as the soul's growth in prayer
he leaves nothing to chance. But even in the Exercises
there is abundant evidence of that flexibility and large-
mindedness that are so characteristic of every rule or
letter of direction written by the saint.

Archbishop Goodier, a Jesuit of our own day, is one
of many who have taken up the charge that the Ignatian

way to God cramps the soul. The lucid arguments they advance, drawn from the writings of the saint and his contemporaries, leave no sort of reasonable doubt that "The Ignatian Method" is put forward only tentatively, as one possible means by which to "prepare and dispose the soul" so that it may be ready for whatever God designs to effect in it. "If there is one universal rule in the spiritual life it is this—pray the way *you* find best." So taught Goodier, exponent reliable and attractive of the Ignatian ideal.

The last book written by the archbishop was *Saint Ignatius Loyola and Prayer*. It was unfinished at the time of his death. But the incomplete work was published and shows that St. Ignatius wants his exercitant to become a man of prayer, cost what it may. This objective, so the distinguished author holds, precedes all others. If Ignatius can get his man to enter deeply into prayer, to live and move and have his being in an atmosphere pervaded by the spirit of prayer, he cares little for anything else. Such a person can be depended upon to conquer himself and refuse all parley or truce with inordinate affections. From habitual converse with God he becomes enamored of Him and you may safely assume that his one aim henceforth will be to seek how to love Him and make Him loved.

He warns the director against using undue influence in an affair so sacred as the communication between God and the soul that takes place in prayer. No director should presume to arrogate to himself the role of the Holy Spirit. When the exercitant is praying in order to decide a vocation, the director should "stand in the center like a balance and leave the Creator to act immediately with the

creature, and the creature with its Creator and Lord."
The exercitant too must be exceedingly sensitive to the
touchings of God on his soul in prayer. He should never
be in a hurry to flit from one point to another in prayer,
but should rest in that place where his soul seems to find
its God. Prayer is a loving conversation between God and
the soul. Ignatius would warn his exercitant against mo-
nopolizing the conversation when God would speak Himself, or of forcing another subject of conversation if the
divine majesty indicates one different.

It is excellent to prepare beforehand the subject matter
for the conversation, preferably at night with a view to
using it in the morning's audience with God. Let the exercitant turn it over quietly in his mind while going to
bed and train himself to recall it first thing in the morning.
It may be a scene from the Gospel, or merely a few words
of a text. Let him be free here as in all else to select for
himself what he judges most suited for his own spiritual
needs.

The saint is most insistent on what he calls "the usual
preparatory prayer." He wants you, before you start
praying, first to stand and steady your mind for a minute
or two, trying to realize what exactly it is you are about
to do. He would have you "place yourself in the presence
of God" Of course you are always in that presence,
whether you think of it or not. But what he wants is that
at the beginning of your prayer you make an act of conscious advertence to it, and follow this up with an offering of yourself and all your powers "that they may all be
ordered singly to God's glory and honor." He would
have you put yourself unreservedly in His hands, reiterat-

ing Mary's "fiat" and expecting that in you too He who is mighty will do great things in prayer.

That imagination of yours is like a restless child. Mother will give the child a toy to occupy it, and if the child lets the toy fall mother will pick it up and hand it back again. Place before your imagination a picture that will restrain its wanderings, and if during the course of the meditation it loses hold, quietly but firmly call it back to that scene again.

It is good to set before you some definite objective to hope for as a result of this period alone with God. It may be deeper sorrow for sin, or more intimate knowledge and love and closer imitation of Jesus Christ; it may be grief with Him in His sufferings or joy with Him in His victories—all according to the subject matter on which you are meditating.

Now quietly think over a portion of the matter you read last night. By all means have the book near you to refresh your memory. Get the will going as soon as you can in acts of love, desire, petition, according as the action of grace affects your soul. You will be weary enough at times. The temptation will come along that you should curtail the period you originally intended to spend in prayer. In such a case not only should you spend the full time, but increase it. Instead of cutting off ten minutes add on five. Thus you not only resist the devil but you take up the offensive against him and overthrow him. In these few extra minutes our generous God will often reward the soul with much light and consolation.

At the same time you are not to estimate the worth of your prayer by what you feel. Feelings of sweetness and satisfaction are excellent and there is no reason why we should not ask for them—with absolute dependence on the divine will. But prayer that is devoid of any particle of comfort may be in reality much more conducive to God's glory, and here as in everything else this is the saint's only criterion of true success.

These are mere gleanings from his teaching about prayer, meant to show that he was no rigid believer in one hard-and-fast method. They also make clear that his main concern is to have the soul in a state of preparedness, to keep it thus, ever ready, in loving expectancy of whatever action God may deign to communicate to it. There is a form of prayer which St. Teresa compares to rain falling from heaven. We cannot have the rain just whenever we want it. But we can plough the ground and sow the seed; we can then confidently hope that our loving Father will send the rain in due season.

In prayer the soul gives and in prayer the soul receives. Unless it gives it will not receive. What it gives is important, essential indeed for a life of prayer. But Ignatius, speaking again from the book of personal experience, knows well that what it receives surpasses in value what it gives immeasurably more than all the treasures in the bank surpass a single copper coin.

Foremost amongst the more excellent gifts given by God is a sense of His presence which tends to become more and more habitual. "That man prays very little," wrote Blessed Father de la Colombière, "who prays only on his knees." This spirit of prayer which is virtually uninterrupted was exceedingly dear to the heart of Ignatius. He did not encourage his students to spend long periods in prayer, but he insisted that they should go to God through their studies. "In all things let them seek

God." For the men who had completed their period of training in his Society he refused consistently, though many times importuned, to assign any particular period of time for them in which to pray.

Assuredly his reason was not that he undervalued prayer or was not concerned about their prayer. On the contrary, as we have been contending, on prayer he set the highest price and like St. Thomas would measure the success of all apostolic work by the interior spirit of prayer and union with God of which it is, or should be, the expression. But he left his men free to pray when and how they could because he was persuaded that if they had understood him aright and had been formed as he willed them to be formed, they would have a veritable thirst for prayer. They would turn to it instinctively, knowing its necessity and having tasted its sweetness. To borrow a phrase of his from another context, he would consider that where prayer was concerned they would need "the curb rather than the lash."

To this day full scope is given to the formed Jesuit who is drawn by God's grace to spend much time in formal prayer. The principle is laid down by Father Aquaviva, one of the Fathers General, and quoted by one of his very recent successors. "If anyone is able to assure himself that he will not hurt his health by excessive application, nor fail in his duties to others, nor show himself less prompt in carrying out the orders of Superiors with becoming alacrity, he is then left free, with no less credit than merit to himself, to devote to earnest meditation or reading whatever time he can spare for his own progress in perfection, provided, however, that in each case one's confessor be consulted, and that, in case of doubt as to what is best, the matter be referred to the Superior."

Different souls are differently attracted by the Spirit of God. Ignatius is not so much worried as to whether a man spends a great deal of time on his knees or not. What more than all else he looks for is that spirit of detachment or renunciation by which a man readily adapts himself to any circumstances, careful above all to seek God in them, to find Him in them, to supernaturalize his relations with them, and thus to learn the supreme art of praying always.

XI

CHRIST OR ANTICHRIST

UNDOUBTEDLY Ignatius had a *penchant* for scenes of apostolate where humanly speaking there was peculiar difficulty and special need. Germany's great apostle, the Jesuit St. Peter Canisius, who saved the faith in that country, has written a sentence which, says Father Broderick his biographer, "should stir a Jesuit's blood like the music of trumpets." Here it is: "The more afflicted and even the more desperate things are in the opinion of the world, the more will it be our part to come to the rescue of forlorn hopes, precisely because we are of the Society of Jesus."

It is said that while Ignatius was in Manresa he learned in prayer that God willed him to found an Order, the Order or Company of Jesus. In that period of prolonged prayer and withdrawal from the noise and distraction of the world he saw the ideal man as required for that Order. Much that he saw and learned he embodied in an immortal meditation which he called "Two Standards."

As you read it over you are inclined to touch the page with the tips of your fingers and then examine them to see if the ink is yet dry. So up-to-the-minute is this meditation, written four hundred years ago, that you might easily enough believe it had just come forth, straight from the hands of its author. Like so much more in his book,

"Two Standards" is meant to be made the subject matter of your thought, not merely to be read over like an essay to interest or entertain. And he wants no mere superficial thinking. Here he places before you a series of momentous facts which he has marshaled, to turn over in your mind prayerfully, profoundly, noting every detail he has inserted. Always a realist, he poses the practical question: In the light of these facts what is to be done? In the light of these facts what are you to do? What are you going to do? Pray intensely for the grace you need to do it, whatever will most redound to the greater glory of God.

If you are to benefit to the full by what he proposes to put before you, he would have you, at the start, isolate yourself as completely as possible from alien subjects. On the threshold, before he permits you to open the text, he reminds you of "the usual preparatory prayer." You are once more going to enter into God's audience chamber, to speak to God and let God speak to you. Steady that restless imagination of yours, call home those wandering thoughts and offer to God a holocaust of all your powers of mind and heart and body, that they all may be employed exclusively for the service and praise of God. It might help you to stand, at this stage, a little distance from the place where you are going to pray. As you make this preparatory prayer, perhaps you might join your hands and close your eyes in the serious effort to gather all your powers together and focus them on the thought of the God to whom you are about to speak.

It is certain that much failure in prayer can be traced to slipshod beginnings. Whatever distractions you may have as the prayer advances, there is no one but can, with God's grace, make this preparation, and Ignatius considers that a good beginning goes a long way to ensure true success.

He now proceeds to unfold before your eyes the vision vouchsafed to him in the cave at Manresa. Look out on your modern world, he would say, and observe how at this moment it is sharply divided into two camps—on the one side Lucifer, bearer of false light, on the other Jesus Christ who enlightens every man coming into this world. Each of the two wants to win the entire world, nothing less, and enlist all men under his respective standard. Is not this the exact issue today between the Church of Jesus Christ and the leaders of communism? Each wishes and desires to win the world—Christ to lead all men to heaven, communism to build a heaven on this earth and ruthlessly to exterminate any who dare oppose its ideals.

The next step is to betake yourself to the camp of Satan and see at close range what is there being done. The leader is seated on a lofty throne of smoke and fire, horrible and terrifying to look upon. All this is indicative of the boastfulness of the Evil One, of his pride, of the confusion and restless agitation that reign in his kingdom, of his hideous appearance, angelic beauty disfigured thus by sin. "How art thou fallen from heaven, O Lucifer, who didst rise in the morning!" [1]

Who can fail to recognize here much that is suggestive of the program and tactics of modern communism? Who does not know that the leaders of communism strive to keep their underlings constantly occupied, ceaselessly active, thus to preclude the possibility of sitting back and dispassionately and objectively examining the claims and ideals of communism? Men who have suffered at the hands of communism do not hesitate to state that the

energy and zeal of its apostles may fairly be described
as satanic.

Satan has his minions, "innumerable demons," says St.
Ignatius, whom he dispatches on missions throughout the
whole world. No country or city may they allow to
escape them, no little village, no individual even is to be
omitted. If Satan's Enemy will assign a special angel to
guard each single soul, Satan too will commission one
of his horde to labor for the ruin of one particular soul
at a time. Every individual counts. Every man is a brick,
a cog in the machine.

Before they set out Satan calls them together for a ha-
rangue. His commands are issued in harsh bullying tones.
They are received in sullen silence. This tyrant exacts
blind unquestioning obedience. Each serf in the ranks is
to follow the party line—theirs not to reason why, theirs
but to do or die. Despite their contempt of the leader the
whole mob is prepared to carry out his orders with metic-
ulous exactness, for all of them have this in common—
hatred of God and the iron resolve to filch from Him
the souls redeemed by the Blood of His Son. What are
Satan's tactics? His emissaries are to cast out nets and
chains, ensnaring men without letting them suspect the
deceit. Just as a fish or a bird does not realize that it is
caught in the net or the snare till it tries to get away, so
these poor men will be doped and duped and entangled
hopelessly, all ignorant of their condition till they are
finally dragged into hell.

Stir up their desire for wealth, Satan advises. Persuade
them to turn their eyes downward toward this earth, not
to any vague hereafter. Fire them with ambition. Make
them avid for power. That is the way to feed their pride,

and if you succeed in leading them to unbounded pride the prize is all but yours.

Is Ignatius in the sixteenth century writing a history of the twentieth? And if his blunt references to Satan and hell seem almost naïve to our sophisticated minds, may we not suggest that his realism is an indictment and a challenge to our modern cynicism? Satan exists. Hell is a stark fact. There is a war on. It is madness to bury your head in the ground and like the ostrich tell yourself everything is all right. You cannot be neutral. It is Christ or antichrist. "He who is not with me is against me, and he who does not gather with me scatters." [2]

You will heave a sigh of relief as you come from this oppressive atmosphere of darkness and hatred out into the glorious sunshine, much as many a poor liberated prisoner has sighed on stepping from behind the Iron Curtain. St. Ignatius would now have you go on your knees, or if you prefer, stand erect, in reverence before Jesus Christ. Him you find not on any lofty throne but down in a lowly place, meek and humble of heart, most winning to look upon, fairest among the sons of men. Here there is no bragging, no haggling; the sullen silence of Satan's camp is replaced by the devoted love which no one who knows Him can withhold from his leader.

As you enter His camp He fixes His eyes upon you and even this first gaze from Him confirms you in the conviction that He and He alone is worth all your love, all the sacrifice, all the labor you ever expended and ever can expend, in executing whatever he demands. This is no mere earthly beauty; this Man is God in the flesh, and divinity seems to flash through the veils of His sacred humanity.

Do you see who those are who will henceforth be your companions? You are privileged to rub shoulders with saints and martyrs, ancient and modern. Apostles and disciples of every age drew from Christ, standing there in their midst, inspiration that swept aside every obstacle, fired with one mighty ambition—to spend itself and be spent selflessly in His divine service and praise. Missioners are here around Him—Peter and Paul, Augustine and Benedict and Francis, Ignatius and Xavier, Claver, Patrick, Columba, Vincent de Paul. Valiant women too like Teresa, Bridget, Thérèse of Lisieux, drew from Him that love that seemed to intoxicate them with joy and translated itself into deeds. Laymen and laywomen—Ozanam, Matt Talbot, Maria Goretti, Edel Quinn—you will find them in the ranks here, their example a source of courage, their work for the salvation of the world a reproach to our apathy.

Here is where you belong—with Christ, under the standard of Christ, associated most intimately with men and women distinguished in His service, who gladly gave all in the excess of their love, in many cases even the greatest proof of all that they laid down their lives for Him. Every Catholic worthy of the name is an apostle.

To you also He deigns to entrust a mission. The honor of it! The responsibility of it! On you He wills to depend to spread abroad among all classes and peoples His sacred doctrine. Tell the world what He tells you. Convince the world that He and He alone is worthwhile, the one abiding, enduring reality in a universe constantly vacillating. Open the eyes of the world, blinded by deceits and snares, and show it what it is missing through ignorance of Him. You are a worker in a factory—tell your fellow workers.

You are a parent in a family—tell your children. You are a teacher in school—seize on the precious opportunities afforded you in your profession to tell those boys and girls. You are unemployed—do not be idle; if you have caught the flame of love from the Sacred Heart, you will discover ways and means to communicate it to others.

XII

PLAN OF CAMPAIGN

Antichrist is reincarnate in modern communism and Christ unconquered opposes him still. This is clear from even the brief summary we gave of what St. Ignatius has to say in "Two Standards."

At first sight it seems strange that nowhere in his book does the saint direct us to pray for zeal. Assuredly this is not because he undervalued zeal or thought that genuine apostleship is possible without it. With all his great heart and soul he would endorse the burning exhortations of our Holy Father bidding us bestir ourselves and win the world back to God.

What he does tell us to beg for in this meditation is not zeal, but true humility—or rather, the virtues that will culminate in humility. We pray often enough for the possession or restoration of a virtue—chastity, patience, charity, temperance. St. Ignatius would wish us to beg not so much for any specific virtue as for the means that will make for the acquiring of that virtue, and the grace to employ those means. This is more fundamental. We would all wish to have the virtue, but we are slow enough to use the means. We would wish to be pure, but at the same time to be free to frequent the occasion of our sin. We would gladly have patience but do not like the self-discipline which must be exacted as the price of patience.

Here too Ignatius, ardently desiring to fill our hearts
with zeal for Christ and souls, tells us to beg for the means
which will foster zeal rather than for zeal itself. Indeed
he does not mention zeal at all. What he does want us to
acquire is humility. He knows that God resists the proud
but gives grace to the humble. Hence, he would say, beg
for the virtues that will lead you to profound and sincere
humility, and zeal will then look after itself.

In point of fact, study of the men most distinguished
for zeal proves them in every case to be rooted and
founded in true self-knowledge—which is another name
for humility. Under His standard none will be accepted
except those who are humble, or who are prepared to
make full use of the means that develop humility.

What then are these means? The first step is poverty,
at least poverty in spirit, which, while perhaps possessing
material things is detached from them in the heart. He
has had much to say about this detachment, right from
the beginning when he explained to us the use of *creatures*. But the soul captured by the love of Christ is
reluctant to practice poverty only in spirit. It thirsts for
actual poverty such as He had. It is aware that such
poverty, despised by the purse-proud of the world, can
advance the soul with giant strides towards humility. This
doctrine is simply the First Beatitude: "Blessed are the
poor in spirit, for theirs is the kingdom of heaven." [1]

If you are poor, prepare for hard knocks. Not much
consideration will be shown a poor man, not much care
for his susceptibilities, even from persons from whom he
has a right to expect it. Often his lot may be plenty of
scorn, contempt, a feigning not to see or notice him, a
deliberate ignoring of a suggestion he makes, even of his

very presence. Human nature resents all this, but in all such things the apostle being formed in the school of Ignatius finds grist for his mill.

Contradictions, insults, bitter complaints against him, lies and calumnies, failures, snubs, misrepresentation—if he can learn to accept these sweetly, they will contribute mightily to the developing of humility, and humility is the basic virtue needed for Christ's apostle. Easy? No one ever said it was. Nature's way is to break out in loud expostulations and complaints, to furnish lengthy explanations, to recount every detail and show how unjust it is, sometimes to vow vengeance and resolve to get its own back. The humble soul prefers to keep silence. It has found a treasure, a hidden treasure of great price. Hidden it remains. If it were exposed it might easily die; at least it would fade and lose the freshness and fragrance it now possesses.

Only those who are genuinely humble will God use as instruments in the work of the apostolate. If souls seem sometimes to be converted or affected for good by those who are proud, lovers of ostentation, either the conversions are only superficial and passing, or else they are brought about by some hidden person, whose prayers and penances, rising up from a humble heart, draw down God's graces.

Hence "Two Standards" concludes with a "triple colloquy." Ignatius leads his exercitant to our Lady and bids him, kneeling at her feet, beg that he might be received under the standard of her divine Son. And does he understand fully the import of his request? He will be received only on the precise terms laid down by Jesus Christ. Only a person keen on growing in humility is a candidate suited to labor for souls by the side of the humble Christ. Am I prepared to adopt the means that will foster humility, or do I merely form a vague desire for this virtue?

Humility demands poverty and detachment in the highest degree of which I am capable. Am I ready to strive to aim at such poverty? Humility calls for acceptance of humiliations, snubs, insults, misunderstandings. Can I rise to the height of sincerely trying to cultivate a love for these? Without these there is no close following of Christ. With these and through these humility grows in the soul, and humility is the seal with which every apostle must be stamped. I end the first part of my colloquy with the *Ave Maria*.

In the company of Mary I come to Christ her divine Son. Once again I kneel and make the same petition, that I may be received under His standard. Once again I have to face the question whether I realize exactly what this acceptance implies. It calls for the love and practice of what is opposed to the cravings of nature—poverty and humiliations which form the sure way to humility, the essential virtue for every apostle. These are His terms. These are the terms I want too. Will He deign to take me and use me on these conditions of His? Having solemnly entered on this engagement I say the *Anima Christi*.

Finally, kneeling with Mary on my left and Christ on my right, I lift up my eyes to my heavenly Father and beg that I may be received under the standard of His divine Son. There is the same questioning and the same reply. This is what I want and desire, and I want it and desire it not on my own conditions but on His. I understand that what I ask is impossible of attainment except by the way of poverty and humiliations. I end my meditation with the *Pater Noster*.

Confirmation of this doctrine is found in the history of our Lord's Baptism. He is just about to enter on His apostolate and He comes to John in poverty and seeks humiliations at his hands. The sinless Son of God would be baptized as though He were a common sinner. John expostulates, but our Lord is insistent. This, He declares, is how to be holy, "to fulfill all justice." "Justice" is synonymous with "sanctity." Hence our Lord teaches that what He is doing is to mark out the road that leads to sanctity. St. Ignatius, who steeped his mind and heart and soul in every detail of the Man-God, does not fail to observe the poverty and humiliation and the truth that Christ emphasizes—that they lead to humility and that only those who are humble are fitted to be received under His standard.

So concerned is the saint to have us grasp this doctrine that he goes on to devote another meditation to humility, explaining its degrees and importance and practice. But first he wants to assure himself that he has left no loophole to his exercitant for self-deception. He wants sincerity at all costs, so he checks the dispositions of his disciple and tests his generosity by asking him to consider a parable and apply its lessons to his own correspondence with the movements of grace he is experiencing in his retreat.

XIII

NO COMPROMISE

WHEN St. Paul was urging his disciple Timothy to labor as a good soldier of Christ he recommended to him three ways of approach to the souls he would win. He must be prepared to prove that the doctrine he proposes is such as will appeal to every reasonable man. Hence he must be skilled in the art of meeting intellectual objections and advancing arguments to show how sane is the teaching of Christ.

But it is far from being sufficient that a man be intellectually convinced. He can keep his convictions in cold storage in his mind and, if he does, they will have little or no effect on his practical conduct. Hence Timothy must win the heart to love and enthusiasm for what is seen to be common sense.

For souls who hold back still there is a third method to be applied. Shame them into generosity, teaches St. Paul. Reproach them with their apathy by contrasting it with the devotedness of Christ's friends. Reproach them by recalling the examples of zeal which they see in the world around them in souls consecrated to the apostolate —men and women who have lost everything and in many cases life itself rather than compromise in their allegiance to our Lord and His Church. Reproach them further with

the tireless energy of His enemies who consider themselves highly honored to be asked to make sacrifices.

Argument for the intellect; appeal for the heart and the
will; reproach if either of these fail—so does St. Paul warn
Timothy to gird himself for the work that lies ahead.
"*Argue, Obsecra, Increpa*,"—Reprove; Entreat; Rebuke.

It would be very easy to show how, at the point now
reached in the Exercises, our Lord has been striving to
win the soul by each of these three methods. In the beginning Ignatius has brought the soul face to face with the
fact of creation, from which consideration there must
surely emerge the conclusion that the service of God is
eminently reasonable. Everything is unreasonable except
the life of complete devotedness to Him and His cause.
Then in the "Kingdom" and "Two Standards" there is
a powerful appeal to the will, and there is the reproach
we must experience as we recognize what others have
achieved—those opposed to Him not less than those devoted to the spread of His kingdom.

He has directed us to beg that we may be received
under the standard of Christ. He has warned us that to
enroll under that standard and offer oneself for distinguished service is to let oneself in for trials and the cross.
He has not minimized the conditions, and with full
knowledge and after serious deliberation we have offered
ourselves, protesting that it is our determination to follow
Him closely in detachment from creatures, in spiritual
poverty, in actual poverty too, should He so ordain.

How far are these protestations genuine? This is the
question with which he halts us now. Our promises and
resolutions must be tested on the anvil, and he supplies
the test by bidding us consider three types of men or

women who have heard Christ's appeal, and the different response each of the three gives to it.

Each of the three has an attachment which is not purely for the love of God. St. Ignatius supposes it to be a sum of money, but it might as well be a friendship for another person which is inordinate, or a cherished project which one strives to advance, from motives—possibly hidden—of self-interest. It may be an aversion. Thus St. Margaret Mary had such a horror of cheese that her brother had to stipulate that she should not be asked to eat it in the convent! One day it seemed to her that God was requesting her to overcome this dislike. After a fierce struggle she yielded, "though," she writes, "the sacrifice of my life seemed small by comparison!"

The serious self-examination to which the soul has subjected itself and the light of graces which have been granted must have shown some of the barriers which hinder God's plan. The first type clearly recognizes what is amiss. It sees itself as the cause which hinders the growth of grace and it professes to be grateful for the illuminations given to it. It also proclaims its readiness to rid itself of the obstacle—whatever it be and whatever the sacrifice entailed—but it never gets down to business to put its resolve into practice.

The attitude of this soul reminds one of the person who owes a sum of money and is all the time assuring himself and others that he intends to pay. But he passes out of this world and the debt is still owing. The soul who has reached the present point in the Exercises, if it has made them in the dispositions called for by St. Ignatius, must undoubtedly have learned a new sense of values. But it procrastinates, always resolving and never doing, and death finds it still hesitating, still afraid to make the sacrifice. This is the basest metal of all.

St. Augustine dallied thus for a time. "Give me chastity, O Lord," he prayed, "but not yet!"

The second type also sees what is hindering it from entire devotedness to Christ. It would like to be freed from this attachment, and vaguely hopes that this freedom may some day be gained. Meantime it will do other things. The Lord, so to say, holds His index finger underneath the one real obstacle that is blocking the soul's spiritual progress. The soul pretends not to see—will promise to give alms, to undertake extra prayers or fasts, to enroll in Legion or Sodality work. But *this?* What will the soul do about *this*—the obstacle indicated by the finger of God, the sacrifice demanded, the change which is clearly demanded by the divine will? *This?* The soul does not hear or see *this*. Anything else, but surely God cannot be asking for *this?*

If only God would come the soul's way instead of asking the soul to come His way! If divine grace would only not be so ruthless and so uncompromising! Thus, the second type of soul refuses to correspond with the invitations of Christ and remains at best mediocre. It has a mere velleity to follow Him closely, not a determination, no real wish. It goes on fooling itself, throwing dust in its own eyes; there are none so blind as those who refuse to see. "There are souls," wrote Père Lallemant, "who spend years, sometimes an entire lifetime, bargaining with God."

One is reminded here of the teaching of St. John of the Cross. He spares no trouble to prove how inordinate desires foil the divine designs. They cause agitation, blindness, hardness of heart, ignorance of the movements of grace. One remembers the lament of St. Teresa that souls advance generously, but only up to a certain point. Through natural diffidence, or wrong spiritual direction, through infidelity to grace, they weaken and turn back on the road to sanctity. St. John of the Cross in particular expresses the anguish he feels that so many souls, just at the very time when God is beginning to purify them with a view to immense progress in solid virtue, presently withdraw themselves from His action and settle down to a comfortable mediocrity.

It would be interesting to compare the teaching of these two great Carmelite mystics with that of St. Ignatius, more especially concerning this second type of soul which "bargains with God."

The third soul hears the appeal of Christ and sees what the obstacle is which opposes His action. God wants *this* —a sacrifice, a different work to do, a different place to live, a resentment long cherished to be immolated. "This" can take many forms. But this third soul, on seeing what God wills, instantly gives it, and with both hands. There will be pain in the giving, a struggle, a temptation to listen to the sophistries of the second type, but all these are resisted. Why? Simply because it does really love Christ, and love is not a matter of sentiment merely, but of deeds. Once convinced that God is asking for the sacrifice it girds itself to give it, and at once. It even likes to consider itself as having already made it, already yielded to the divine invitations. "There must be no reserves in love."

You will agree that Ignatius is taking no risk. He leaves no loophole for compromise or self-deception. "If you really love," he would say, "learn that love, divine love, calls for all—even *this*." But he has not yet sounded the possible depths of self-deception. He has still a note to add, another charge of dynamite to our self-complacency.

We might introduce his note perhaps by contemplating briefly our Lord's prayer in Gethsemani. On Holy Thursday night He knelt under the shadow of the olive trees in preparation for the sufferings of the Passion. The words He uttered make it clear that His human nature recoiled with horror from the ordeal that lay ahead in the immediate future. But "falling into an agony, he prayed the more earnestly" [1] and steeled Himself to accept the bitter chalice presented to His lips. "Not my will but thine be done." [2]

St. Ignatius in his anxiety to preserve us from anything that might lessen or weaken the totality of our dedication challenges us at this point to ask ourselves if there is any "chalice" for which we, like Christ, feel an instinctive repugnance. Most of us will discover things we naturally shrink from. An unpleasant person who is likely to come and spend several weeks in our home—and we definitely do not want that person. A difficult job that has to be done—and we hope somebody other than ourselves will be picked for it. Extra work that is pending, and whoever undertakes it will have to sacrifice all his free afternoons —and no increase in salary.

Or there may be something to which we are inordinately attached, and our natural reaction in this case is to hope from our heart that nobody will think of suggesting we give it up. We cherish a pet scheme; we are exceedingly anxious that nothing should occur to interfere with our arrangements; we find ourselves inclined to defend with too much vigor, perhaps with acrimony, our views in politics, and we lack all tolerance for those who disagree.

What would St. Ignatius advise in order to ensure that we divest ourselves entirely of self-love? Why, he would have us beg in our prayers, even though it be against the grain, that God would give us the very thing we are fearful of, or take away what we naturally dread to lose, "provided only it be to the service and praise of the divine goodness." Always the same criterion—the greater glory of God. If God will be more glorified by the sacrifice of what I naturally cling to, or by the acceptance of what I dislike so heartily—then, for Ignatius, there is no more to say. This only would he add—as a guaranty against all possible deception—incline rather by preference towards what you naturally dislike. It is the safer course. Indeed it will be well if you beg God to give you what is against your inclination, or take from you what you are fearful of giving up.

There will not be much warmth, much feeling of enthusiasm, it is true, in such a prayer. You may even feel you are insincere, that you really do not want what you ask. But it is the effort of the will that is above all pleasing to God. The difficult struggle that the doing costs is enormously sanctifying, much more so than any amount of sensible sweetness and feelings of consolation.

Whether God wills to accept this petition we make or not is not yet certain. What Ignatius wants to secure is that the soul will kneel before Him ready for whatever may most glorify the divine majesty. He would have the soul work itself, as much as possible, into the frame of mind that considers that the sacrifice it contemplates is already made, that God has already asked it. The soul tries to envisage itself as having already abandoned the thing in actual fact. It has no intention of going back to it again unless God clearly shows that this course is for His greater glory.

A Jesuit was once giving the Exercises to a religious community. When he came to this difficult note he did not spare his hearers. One man squirmed in his place. He had a position in his community which he detested and he had made up his mind to ask for a change. After that lecture he went down on his knees and prayed that he might *not* be changed. He sweated in the effort. There was not a particle of consolation in that prayer.

Christ sweated in Gethsemani too.

XIV

BEDROCK

A FEW chapters back we quoted Father Alvarez de Paz to the effect that God and a truly humble soul are both omnipotent—the One to give and the other to receive.

Satan's objective is to lead the soul to unbounded pride, a sort of swelling of self-consciousness, in which the idea of "self" becomes overgrown. Get the soul immersed in anything outside of God, he orders, not necessarily anything sinful. For a start it is enough that it become absorbed in work even, in organizations, in study, in a hobby that is harmless in itself. All you want at this point is that the object become as much an obsession as possible.

Stir up the soul to desire the limelight, to seek popularity, to talk much about the real good it does. No need for bludgeoning the soul, pretend you are going its way, lead it on by deceits, trap it by nets and chains—little by little—keeping your eye all the while on the goal, unbounded pride.

What a toll this program has taken, and continues to take, in wrecking the human race, soul and body! Bishop Fulton Sheen has calculated that in 3,358 years there were 227 years of peace, and 3,130 years of war—thirteen years of war for every one year of peace! Within the last three centuries there have been 286 wars in Europe. From

1500 B.C. to A.D. 1850 there were 8,000 treaties of peace which were supposed to remain in force forever. The average length of these treaties was two years.

Since 1100 England has spent half of its history fighting wars; France nearly half; Russia three-quarters.

Unbounded pride is at least the partial explanation of this doleful record. That is why Ignatius will have men to excel in humility. Humility is a most true knowledge of oneself in the clear light of which one recognizes one's own worthlessness. Humility does not mean ignorance of the gifts with which God may have endowed me. Still less is it the affected self-depreciation of Uriah Heap. If a man has gifts, a sane humility shows him that he has them for one only reason—simply because God saw fit to entrust them to him. "What hast thou that thou hast not received, and if thou hast received it, why dost thou boast as if thou hadst not received it?" [1]

Recognizing thus his dependence on God and his indebtedness to Him, the humble man submits himself, subjects himself to God, and St. Ignatius finds three ways by which he does so. There is first the man who humbles himself before God in the case where God commands under pain of mortal sin. This is the man's habitual frame of mind. He may, it is true, sometimes fall into grave sin, but he will repent at once. Ordinarily, says St. Ignatius, if he were to be made lord of all created things he would not deliberate about committing a mortal sin; this frame of mind he maintains even at the cost of his life.

This is the disposition necessary for a valid absolution from mortal sin. The penitent's purpose of amendment demands that he be determined to avoid all serious sin, and insofar as is possible for him, all proximate occasions

that would lead him to such sin. Self-surrender to this
extent is essential for our eternal salvation. "What does it
profit a man if he gain the whole world but suffer the loss
of his own soul? Or what will a man give in exchange for
his soul?" [2]

The second kind of humility goes farther than the first.
Here there is no question of the commission of sin, even
venial. In this second degree the soul habitually shuns
every deliberate venial sin, and mortal sin is completely
ruled out. Further, when the soul is faced with a choice—
how to spend its time, for example—it reaches its decision
by the measuring rod of God's will and His glory. It
professes itself resigned in all things to the eternal decrees,
and in actual practice it lives consistently with this profession.

Suppose a person in this second kind of humility is
seriously ill, threatened with a painful and critical operation. His prayer will be like the prayer of Job: "As it shall
please the Lord so let it be. Welcome be the will of God.
If God send pain and death, may His will be done!" If
on the other hand He sends relief and a complete recov-
ery, the soul will accept it gratefully and bless Him for
that too.

This is the detachment or indifference about which
St. Ignatius had so much to say in the first week. We
might easily imagine that subjection to God can go no
farther. It is most true that a soul who lives habitually in
this spirit of unquestioning resignation is fervent and sincere in its service of God.

But Ignatius discovers yet a further degree of humility.
Enamored as he was of Jesus Christ, the most ardent longing of his heart was to become more and more like Him.

Now everyone knows that Christ our Lord deliberately chose for Himself a life of poverty and suffering. This He did not because poverty and suffering were necessary in order to accomplish our salvation. A single prayer would have been more than sufficient to redeem us. But He did not will to confine Himself to what was strictly necessary. Why not? Simply because love is not like that. Professions of love ring truest when they translate themselves into deeds of self-sacrifice.

True love seeks what it can give. There is an ugly counterfeit which looks only for what it can get.

Hence the soul in the third degree of humility is habitually prejudiced in favor of whatever is difficult, or painful, or humiliating. Place a choice before such a soul. Two courses are open before it, one is naturally pleasant and the other demands self-sacrifice. To make the case concrete, let me suppose that this evening you are free either to read a book in which you are deeply interested, or to visit a poor old man who is ill, garrulous, deaf, full of self-pity, utterly uninteresting.

If you settle down to your good book, and do so with a right intention, your action is meritorious in God's sight. The book is informative, stimulating, written in a graceful style, and you enjoy it thoroughly. By reading it this evening you glorify God. "For those who love God all things work together unto good." [3] Your two hours' reading gives, let us say, sixty degrees of external glory to God.

If on the other hand you reluctantly lay aside your book and visit the old man, you will perform an act which you distinctly dislike. You find conversation boring and difficult with this querulous person. You know that he will treat you to a litany of complaints. He will not thank you for coming. He will assume as a matter of course that you will stay two hours listening to his diatribes, that you will give him money, that you are prepared to execute any number of petty orders, unimportant to everyone except himself.

Still you decide to go, though you long for that book. If you do go, you give to God a certain measure of external glory. How much? St. Ignatius says sixty degrees, exactly the same as you would have given had you followed your natural inclination. Whether this would be so in actual practice is unlikely, but it is important to observe that he lays it down as a working hypothesis.

What will the soul do that lives habitually in the spirit of the third kind of humility? If the two courses of action were to give the same glory to God, there could be only one answer. Unquestionably it will take what is hard. The tempting volume will deliberately be closed, and two hours will cheerfully be spent at the sick man's bedside. But why? Why not take the pleasant thing if it is going to give the same glory to God as the hard thing? Once more there is the spontaneous reply: "What is hard makes me more like to Christ. He walked the hard way by deliberate choice. That is the way for me too."

Will the generous soul *always* choose what is hardest? One has been privileged to know such souls who invariably rejected whatever was pleasant and easy to human nature and always, it seemed, took by deliberate preference what was hard and painful. St. John of the Cross, kneeling before the image of Christ crucified, heard the Master say: "John, you have served me well. What reward can I give you?" The answer is sublime: "Reward,

Lord? One only reward do I seek—to suffer and to be despised for Thy sake."

The votary of the world faced with a sacrifice asks: "Why *should* I make it? Why should *I* be picked on for this suffering? Why not somebody else undertake this unpleasant job?" The exercitant who has absorbed the teaching of Ignatius says: "Why should I *not?* This is what I am after—anything that goes against my natural love of ease, my natural tendency to slacken, to pass on to another what I dislike. Here it comes to me—why should I *not* reach out and take it eagerly?"

There is a whole world of difference between the two attitudes. The person schooled in the third kind of humility is reluctant to allow any chance of sacrifice to slip through his fingers. But though he has this bias in favor of what is hard, the conclusion does not follow that he will *always* take it. When will he take by deliberate preference the easier, more pleasant course? When he sincerely believes that in certain circumstances the pleasanter thing will give to God, not the same glory as the hard thing, but *greater* glory. "When the fire is lit," wrote St. Francis de Sales, "we see that obedience would have us warm ourselves, provided it be not done with too much eagerness."

This is quite consistent with the Ignatian doctrine on the third degree of humility. There will be cases where the soul chooses the pleasanter course, but it chooses not merely because this is what it naturally likes, but because it is convinced that here is an instance where it must forgo, almost reluctantly, what is hard, because in this particular instance the easier thing will glorify God more.

In applying this doctrine two dangers have to be

guarded against. Characters are very different and there are some who, if they were to take too literally what is here laid down, might become morbid, unduly introspective. In general it may be said that if a course of action makes a person gloomy and morbid, that person is on wrong lines. "God loves a cheerful giver." [4] If a person were always to be analyzing his motives, always weighing up which course is more for God's glory—in the trivial matters of everyday living—he might suffer injury. Hence for such a one it would be for God's greater glory that he should not overanalyze. Let him cultivate a general intention of seeking God in all things, renew it often, and after that accept simply as from His hands whatever comes along whether it be pleasant or unpleasant.

The second danger is one that has more than once been emphasized by our Holy Father. It is the rejection in practice of all asceticism on the plea that love of God alone matters, and one can accept all the pleasant things that are offered—and seek them—provided this is done in the spirit of gratitude and love. There is no need to do anything hard, certainly anything over and above a conscientious discharge of duty. When duty is done, relaxation comes, so take all the natural enjoyments you can get, offer them to God and be grateful to Him for giving them to you. The Ignatian ideal of the third degree is right enough in its way, but it must be interpreted and adapted to suit the needs of our time.

On the morning after he proclaimed the Dogma of the Assumption, Pius XII assembled the cardinals and bishops, nearly six hundred of them, for a special audience. One of the points he stressed was the terrifying success of communism and the evil it is doing to the souls redeemed by

Christ. The Holy Father offered an explanation for this success. He deplored the lack of this precise spirit of penance in the Church today—which Ignatius teaches under the heading of the third degree of humility—and to the lack of this spirit and practice he attributed the triumphs of God's enemies.

Our Lady's message at Lourdes was: Penance. Penance. Penance. At Fatima she asked not only that the Rosary should be recited, but also—what we tend to overlook—that sacrifices should be made.

It is true that too rigid an interpretation of the doctrine of the third degree may have its dangers. It may lead to spiritual pride. It may take all joy out of the spiritual life—"no cake and ale because I am good!" It may develop a tendency to contempt for others who perhaps consider that ascetical practices are out of date. The objection may be made that mere asceticism will not make a man love God, and love is all that God values. These are objections which may not be lightly dismissed. But they are answerable, and it is the business of the spiritual director to show that they are more specious than real.

One would like to point out that the course which goes habitually the easy way, and justifies it on the plea that it is the expression of one's love of God, also abounds in dangers. One sometimes has the uncomfortable feeling that St. Paul might stigmatize those who follow it as "enemies of the cross of Christ!" [5] One wonders if the advocates of this way are sufficiently cognizant of the fact of original sin. We have a fallen nature only too ready to compromise, too ready to tone down the "hard sayings" of the Gospel. Is this the explanation of the complaint about the dearth of really spiritual men and women? Is this why the Sacred Heart told St. Margaret Mary that He was treated with coldness and contempt even by those consecrated to Him?

"Unless the grain of wheat falls into the ground and dies, it remains alone. But if it dies, it brings forth much fruit." [6] Self-love, it has been said, dies a quarter of an hour after the soul departs from the body.

St. Ignatius is putting high doctrine before us in all this. He was convinced in his day that the world was starving for idealism. It is starving still, starving in the midst of plenty.

XV

MANRESA AGAIN

AT Manresa St. Ignatius experienced an invasion of his soul by divine grace. All his previous ideals were shattered. He seemed to himself like a man who, born blind, had received for the first time the inestimable gift of sight. That is why he yearns to have every exercitant become a man of prayer. It was in prayer that he himself learned all; heavenly lights and revelations were given to him in abundance, and he is well aware that these are still awaiting the person who takes the life of prayer seriously. The Heart of Christ, from which he drew them, is an inexhaustible source. "If *anyone* thirst, let him come to me and drink." [1]

A Poor Clare writes: "The call to live is the call to live for God. The vocation to life and the vocation to prayer are one and the same, and to the loving soul vocation is an inebriation, for it is the call of the divine lover. 'Behold, I have created thee, and redeemed thee, and now thou art and prayest me.'

"My God, how awe inspiring a preparation for the prayer of the soul! Countless ages and the sublime dramas of creation and redemption culminate in the union of the soul with God. Lord, 'what is man that you should be mindful of him?' [2] for nothing seems too great to satisfy the demands of Thy mighty love. The whole universe is not too vast a setting for that silent, hidden, encounter between any one tiny soul and the Eternal Trinity. In a sense all creation leads up to it."

Again: "To each soul belongs the responsibility of the power to add by what the soul is to the sum of all good, or to detract from it. According to the virtue of each one is the standard of the whole. What each soul is interiorly, face to face with God, unknown to anyone, is of vital consequence to all the human race, and every act of love towards God, every act of faith and adoration, every mute uplifting of the heart raises the whole Church, yea the whole world, nearer to God.

"From each soul that is in union with God, and at rest in the divine embrace, radiates a spiritual vitality and light and strength and joy which reaches from end to end of the universe, a source of grace even to those least worthy of it, even to those least conscious of it, and knowing nothing of whence and how it comes."

Truly "more things are wrought by prayer than this world dreams of." Reformation of life always begins with a new perception of some old truth, and it is in the soul's contact with God in prayer that the illumination comes which is at one and the same time shattering and constructive. The invasion by divine grace expels unworthy ideals, sets up new ideals, and shows to the soul in clear light that true success is to be measured only by the fidelity with which it adheres henceforth to these new ideals and propagates them on every side.

"Nothing great or lasting," wrote St. Vincent de Paul, "can be hoped for from those who are ignorant of the art of conversing with God in prayer." "When a man called to promote the salvation of souls," says St. John

Baptist de la Salle, "is filled with the spirit of God, he obtains by prayer all that he desires for the success of his mission."

Such quotations might be multiplied and we have seen that St. Ignatius, like all men who had experienced the joy, the conviction, the love and zeal, which are the fruit of prayer, longed to gather the whole world together and tell them about his discovery. In his prayer Ignatius found Christ. There was the realization of the breath-taking truth that Christ, the Son of the Eternal God, meant just exactly what He said when He assured Ignatius that He loved him! There was the effort to plumb the depths of that fathomless saying of the apostle: "For to me to live is Christ." [3] "It is now no longer I that live, but Christ lives in me." [4] How blind Ignatius had been! Had he been all this while wrapped about in a thick fog, that he had not until now begun to see who and what Christ is? The experience was like that of a man walking up and down a dark room, and being suddenly plunged into brilliant noonday sunshine.

Only a single person can stand at the center of a circle. You can fit ten or ten thousand around the circumference provided you are willing to make the area sufficiently broad. Now Ignatius' dealings with God in prayer confirmed him in the resolution, from which he never afterwards swerved, to put Christ, and Him alone, at the center. In the Litany we invoke our Lord as king and center of all hearts. This is to be His place henceforth in the Ignatian ideal.

Ignatius became enamored of the God-Man to such an extent that the thought of Him and His interests were the only motives to influence every choice, to decide every issue. St. Paul had written: "Have this mind in you which was also in Christ Jesus." [5] He would have us absorb the mentality of the God-Man. The soul must be so deeply plunged into the love of Christ that it rejoices with Him, grieves with Him, praises God in prayer with Him, and with Him and through Him and in Him offers unceasing homage and thanks to the Eternal Father. "It is now no longer I that live, but Christ lives in me." [6]

This is the climax to which Ignatius would lead the soul. It is perhaps significant that he employs the same word as St. Paul in explaining a cardinal point in the Exercises. St. Paul had written: *sentite*—absorb the mentality of Christ. St. Ignatius warns that it is not the abundance of material placed before the soul to ponder over that will produce best results. What the soul needs is to taste and feel for itself—*sentire et gustare*.

So the soul at all costs must "learn Christ." Ignatius has already brought it face to face with Him in the "Kingdom" and "Two Standards." These are like the wide canvas, but he wants the soul, further, to examine prayerfully and in detail the words of the God-Man, the things He did, the thoughts that filled His divine mind, His gestures however insignificant, His companions—friends and enemies—the places He lived, the disciples He chose, the work to which He called them, the means to be employed. In a word, so obsessed is Ignatius with the conviction that Christ is all that he spares nothing to guide his exercitant to make the discovery for himself.

XVI

A METHOD OF PRAYER

ONE of the methods Ignatius suggests we might perhaps introduce at this point. A way of prayer, he thinks, well worth trying is to select a scene, a "mystery" in the life of our Lord, quietly imagine ourselves as actually moving in the scene ourselves, and prayerfully look at the persons, listen to the words they are saying, and consider the actions they do in this event passing before our eyes. Of course he intends that these three streams of prayerful thinking should flow one into the other. While we are concerned with the persons, for instance, we may at the same time recall what they say and do. The persons, words, and acts, are by no means intended by him to be kept in watertight compartments. But as general headings, as signals giving us broad directions for our praying, as starting points to get our will going in prayer, these three may be found exceedingly useful.

He hopes they may "dispose and prepare the soul" leading it far along that road to intimacy with God which is the goal of all true prayer.

St. John's fourteenth chapter contains this marvelous promise of Christ: "He who loves me will be loved by my Father, and I will love him and manifest myself to him." [1] Questioned by Judas, not the Iscariot, about this "manifestation" he went on to explain that the Blessed Trinity will take up its abode in the soul that loves, dwelling there habitually as a guest, inundating the soul with a joy and a peace which the world cannot give.

This "manifestation" will be the reward of those who know Christ and love Him. No wonder then that Ignatius is so anxious to lead the soul into dispositions that will prove most readily receptive for the communication of the knowledge and love of Jesus Christ.

By way of illustrating the efficacy of the method mentioned a few paragraphs back—of prayerfully contemplating the persons, words, and acts in a given mystery—here is an incident from Père de Caussade, a French Jesuit. He speaks about a poor workingman who used to spend whole hours every evening before the Blessed Sacrament.

"And how do you occupy yourself?" asked the priest.

"The only instruction I ever had on prayer was given to me by my confessor when I was young.

" 'My son,' he told me, 'when you want to pray all you have to do is to place yourself in spirit in some scene of our Lord's life, and speak and think and act exactly as you would do if you were in reality present there.'

"I have taught this simple method to many," the man added, "and I know it has helped them, and by its means they have advanced farther in prayer than I myself."

May we try to show how this method works out in practice? Suppose we take for our scene the Last Supper. We find ourselves in the beginning near the Cenacle, watching our Lord and the twelve as they arrive. There is a stairway outside, leading to the upper story, and we see Him walking up the steps, His long white flowing

garment gathered in His left hand, while with His right
He supports Himself by the railing.

Once inside, the little group begs God's blessing on the
meal, and we do the same. Then we walk up the center,
stand directly opposite Christ, bow with reverence, and
kneel down. He is seated on one side; we are on our knees
on the other side, our joined hands resting on the edge
of the table. From this point of vantage we look at the
persons, listen to their words, watch what they are doing
—and apply all to the needs of our own soul.

Who are the *persons* here? A short while before we
entered, Judas went out to sell his Master; we met him
hurrying with nervous tread along the street below. "It
was night." [2] The terse sentence might well be used to
describe the state of the traitor's soul. If ever a heart is set
on sin it develops a sense of estrangement from those who
retain their devotedness to Christ. It is uncomfortable in
their company, as Judas was uncomfortable tonight. So
he got away, as soon as he could without compromising
himself.

In some such way we continue to contemplate the
different persons, all the while reflecting prayerfully on
ourselves. Our eyes turn to Peter, so full of courage now,
so loud in his protestations of loyalty, so easily frightened
in face of real danger. The rest of the twelve, we look at
one after the other—John with head resting on the Heart
of the Master, Andrew and Philip, James, Bartholomew—
very ordinary persons, chosen for a sublime mission, far
from realizing the dignity to which they are raised as His
apostles, slow to grasp the responsibility of the vocation
He has given them. Such thoughts are not difficult to call
forth as we kneel there, and the will should soon go out in

acts of gratitude—that like them we are called; of sorrow
—that like them we have so often and so sadly failed.

Throughout we are constantly attracted back to look
into the face of Christ. By all means we should follow the
attraction. Speak to Him, speak to them. We do not need
grandiose language. We can employ very simple terms,
expressive of our sorrow, of our anxieties, of our desires
to atone for the past—exactly as we would do if we were
really present there on our knees in front of Christ.

After a while we pause and listen to what they are saying. The entire exquisite discourse of our Lord, as re-
corded at great length by St. John, might occupy our
prayer and prayerful thinking for many a long hour. It is
His farewell talk and every word vibrates with the love
throbbing in the heart of the Speaker. Then, climax of all,
we hear the wondrous words of consecration—"this is
my body . . . this is my blood." [3] We hear the words of
Peter assuring our Lord that even if everyone else proves
false, on Peter at least the Master can depend. And these
are swiftly followed by the solemn warning from Christ
that Peter will deny Him, and three times deny Him, and
this very night deny Him. How much there is to think of
here—our own professions of fidelity, at missions or retreats, in times of illness. When the atmosphere changed
and we found ourselves surrounded—like Peter did later
that same night—by temptation, perhaps temptation of
our own choosing, in this again like Peter, how did we
then stand the test?

What are their *acts?* Our Lord girds Himself with a
towel, takes a basin of water, and actually kneels before
each one to wash the feet of each. How this act of profound humility brings the blush of shame to our face

when we think of our refusal to forgive, even to salute those who have offended us, the eagerness with which we seize on every opportunity to defame the one who has injured us!

Then there is His act of giving them their First Communion, saying the First Mass, ordaining them as His first priests—all summed up in His doctrine and injunction: "This is my body. . . . This is my blood." [4] "Do this in remembrance of me." [5]

We have selected only one scene almost at random to indicate merely how fruitful a method St. Ignatius here suggests to us. It must be clear that the exercitant who would live in this atmosphere, charged with the presence of Christ and lighted up by the example of His life, must soon begin to know Him intimately, and the passage from intimate knowledge to burning love is easy and swift. Only one scene, and with even that we have dealt only very summarily. After that there is the whole Gospel— the Incarnation, Nativity, the hidden life, the preaching, the Passion and Death and Resurrection. A whole lifetime is too short to exhaust it.

This is a way of prayer most suitable for many more souls than try to use it. There are many Catholics who with commendable zeal impose on themselves a lengthy routine of vocal prayers which with painstaking effort they wade through day after day. They do not experience any great joy in the task; it is dry, uninteresting, done in a spirit of hard duty. This is quite certain—that in many cases these well-intentioned souls would pray better, and their prayer would have deeper effect on their own spiritual lives, and it would reach out far farther throughout the Mystical Body to help and heal souls that are ailing and dead, if a change were made.

If the people we have in mind could be induced to curtail the prayers they utter by rote and without attention, "parrot prayers," and learn by degrees some such form of prayer as we are discussing, they would, like Ignatius in Manresa, begin to realize how much they had been missing. They do not see that their obstinacy in clinging to their self-imposed ritual is the result of a subtle pride.

To these Ignatius would say: Do not cut down the amount of *time* you are giving to your long prayers. Spend the same time faithfully each day in prayer, but spend it differently, like Father de Caussade's man, and we can hope that you will share the experience which he assures us happened in his own case, and in the case of many of his friends.

We want substance in our prayer, not a stone but the bread that nourishes. We want depth in our prayer, let us not sacrifice surface to it. We want to pray. We envy the saints who speak, it would seem, from personal experience about the marvels that take place in prayer between God and the faithful soul.

We want to pray. God wants it too. He is much more eager to give us His gifts than we are to receive them. Ignatius is well aware that prayer is a divine science which only a divine Master can teach. Other teachers can "prepare and dispose the soul." Only God can give the increase. He does not give the Spirit by measure.

XVII

A DECISION TO MAKE

LIFE consists in large measure of a series of free choices. You want to contact a friend and you freely decide to write him a letter, or you freely decide to phone. You get an offer of a job and you freely accept it or turn it down. Someone invites you out to dinner, you are asked to join a tennis club or to go with a pilgrimage to Rome, you see a new book in the shop window and you walk inside and freely debate about buying it. In all these cases you come to a decision by freely making up your mind what you are going to do. What are the reasons which determine your choice?

Perhaps you are contemplating marriage and you decide to wait, or you reject the idea, or you go right ahead. You have some idea, it may be, of becoming a priest or a nun, and once more you delay, or try to rid yourself of the notion, or you follow it up all the way. And again the important question: What motives have you for entering the priesthood or the religious state, or if you decide to reject the suggestion, what are your reasons?

St. Ignatius rightly considers that many err seriously here. They make up their minds, for instance, to marry. No doubt they hope to have God's blessing on their union and the saint certainly hopes the same. But he insists all the same that they are getting things mixed up. The end of all living here and hereafter is the perfect loving accomplishment of God's will. Hence, whenever there is a decision to make, whether it be about posting a letter, or marrying, or going to move into a new house, the fundamental question must always be: "What is God's will in the matter?"

What he deprecates is that so many make up their minds *first* to marry, with little or no consideration for the fundamental question, and then, having married, hope that God will prove accommodating and bless the choice, which is now a *fait accompli*. Many choose wrongly because they allow themselves to be governed by passion or impulse, by the prospect of material advantages, such as a home and wealth and comfort. Such considerations need not indeed be excluded, but they are quite secondary in importance and should be given only second place in arriving at a decision. In many cases marriages break down because the contracting parties took on themselves to decide what it was that *they* wanted, and failed to seek in earnest prayer for divine guidance and divine approval. They neglected what must always be the primary consideration: how is this proposed marriage going to affect our eternal salvation?

It is at this stage of the Exercises that St. Ignatius faces us with the "Election" or choice of a state in life. If that choice be made already, what he has to say can easily be applied as a help to living more perfectly according to the duties and ideals of that state. If not, he hopes to give us a few principles to guide us aright in a question of such importance. From all he has taught us so far, the truth must surely emerge that nothing ought to move us except only "the praise and service of God our Lord and the eternal salvation of our souls." Indeed he had said as much on the very title page on which he promises to teach his exercitant how to conquer himself and enable him to put order in his life without being influenced by any inordinate affection.

On the Damascus road Saul knelt and prayed: "Lord, what wilt thou have me do?" [1] Ignatius has his exercitant on the Damascus road now, and he wants this to be his petition too; uttered with deep sincerity and singleness of purpose. Otherwise the person making the choice will "not go straight to God, but will wish rather that God should go straight to him, so that he chooses last what in point of fact he should choose first of all."

Assuming now this basic principle, the saint proceeds to set down a few pertinent and searching questions. Suppose, he says, you had to make this decision for another person, what would you advise him to do? He is a man, say, whom you never met before and whom you are not likely to encounter again. But you would like him to choose what you sincerely believe to be for the good of his soul and for God's greater glory. What are you going to say to him? The saint stipulates that he must be regarded as a complete stranger, so as to ensure that your advice will not be prejudiced in any way. Now, he concludes, do you not think that what you tell him suits yourself admirably?

Or suppose you were on your deathbed. Imagine yourself there now. What decision would you then wish to have made? Or place yourself in spirit before Jesus Christ your judge. Die you certainly will, and you are soon going to stand there. Now is the time to decide what seems best when viewed from the angle of eternity.

A blind old man had for years been a daily communicant. A friendly doctor considered that an operation would restore his sight. He performed it, and very successfully. He warned his patient that if he caught a chill in the eyes he would lose the sight again and there would then be no chance of a further operation.

The old man proceeded to go to his daily Mass and Holy Communion—walking four miles to and from the church each day in all weathers. Of course he got a chill, and of course he lost his sight. The priest remonstrated.

"Father," the old man replied, "let me ask you just one question. When I am being judged, which would I prefer to have to account to God for—the loss of my sight at this age, or the loss of one single Mass and Holy Communion through my own fault?"

The first time when an Election is desirable is when God Himself by His own direct action "moves and attracts the soul." This He did in the case of the apostles and some of the saints. He ordered them to leave their boats and their nets and follow Him. He told the rich young man to rid himself of his money and become His disciple. Such a calling is extraordinary and exceptional and in many cases it would be presumptuous to expect it. More usually God calls and leads the sincere soul to a right decision by means of others—a good director, a chance sermon or reading, an accident which leads to a serious reflection to which the soul has hitherto been unaccustomed.

The exercitant's own personal experiences in prayer furnish a second time useful for an election. Prayer will bring him much light and knowledge and he should test himself to find out what he inclines to do when he feels sweetness and delight in prayer, and what in times of weariness and desolation of spirit. It is further helpful to see what effect each proposed course of action brings about. Perhaps one brings consistently consolation and one persistently disgust. He must then probe further and try to discover the root of this sweetness and the root of the disgust. The feeling for or against must not be accepted as the final criterion. Does it spring from a motive of self-exaltation or fear of self-humiliation? Or is the soul moved in either case by concern for God's greater glory?

There is a third time, a period of tranquillity, when the soul "is not agitated by divers spirits and enjoys the use of its natural powers freely and quietly." At such a time the soul is in the best possible condition to discover God's will. In the ordinary rush of life with its thousand distractions, its incessant claims of work and chatter, the soul finds great difficulty in placing itself in that condition of calm where under the influence of grace it is most responsive to the promptings of God's Holy Spirit. That is why one should be exceedingly slow to tone down one's retreat resolutions on the plea that one was "worked up." The truth is that at such a time one is nearer to the source of divine light than ordinarily, and therefore in a better position to discover God's will in one's regard.

It is not a bad idea, counsels Ignatius, to draw up in writing all the reasons for and against and try to weigh them one with the other, "solely with reference to the praise of our Lord God and the salvation of my soul." All other considerations are beside the mark. That a thing or course of action is pleasing to nature, advantageous or disadvantageous from a merely worldly point of view, is a secondary consideration which should not be permitted to become the deciding factor.

"After such an election has been made he who has made it ought with great diligence to go to prayer in the presence of God our Lord, and to offer Him the said election, to the end that His divine majesty may be pleased to receive and confirm it, if it should be to His greater service and praise."

Finally Ignatius gives the principle which embodies his entire teaching and ideal. "Let each one reflect that he will make progress in all spiritual matters just so far as he shall have divested himself of his self-love, self-will, and self-interest."

What calamities would be averted from nations and individuals if these principles, built on a logic enlightened by grace, were applied in seeking a solution to our problems!

XVIII

A GREAT EFFORT

AT the point now arrived at in the Exercises the retreatant has reached the end of the second week. He has been observing faithfully, "with a large heart," the details of the program mapped out for him by St. Ignatius, and this fidelity has demanded much in the way of self-restraint and self-sacrifice. He has been in his retreat for perhaps seventeen or eighteen days. During this period he has received from his director four or five times each day a short exposition of points for his meditation. This exposition lasted ten or fifteen minutes, not longer, after which he went off alone into complete solitude and there for a full hour or more pondered over prayerfully in his heart what he had listened to.

Further, on several nights he rose for an extra hour of prayer at midnight. He would have submitted to the saint's instructions concerning a close guard of his lips, and heart, and imagination. He would have lived in that absolute "seclusion" which, as we saw, Ignatius regarded as a matter of supreme importance.

Seventeen or eighteen days spent thus would have entailed no small measure of that self-conquest which from the very beginning the exercitant was warned to expect. It has been a strenuous program, and Ignatius assumes that now his disciple may well be somewhat physically fatigued. None the less, so far from promising him some respite, he urges him, as he stands on the threshold of the third week, to brace himself generously for "a great effort." Why?

The third week leads us step by step prayerfully through the events enacted in the course of our divine Lord's Passion and death. Ignatius seems to say to us, in recommending this "great effort": "At all costs you must cooperate here and give of your very best. If you are tired forget your weariness and use if necessary a holy violence against yourself. Whatever you may have missed in the Exercises so far, you must make absolutely certain not to miss this which is now coming along."

A realization of faith of the meaning of the Sacred Passion would shake our souls to their very foundations. Realize the Passion and the realization will set your feet on the road to sanctity as nothing else. Realize the Passion and toying with "creatures" drops out automatically. Full realization indeed is sheer impossibility. Sometimes you have sat in the summer by the seashore. You have watched the great waves coming in, dashing against the rocks, and returning to the ocean. All you see from your place is these few waves, but you know that behind them there is the force and power of the vast expanse, and beneath them the fathomless depths. Saints have made the Sacred Passion the subject matter of their prayer for whole years, for an entire lifetime, only to confess that all they had done even thus far was to watch a few waves, merely to graze the surface. They were vividly conscious of the immense depths still unexplored and remaining of necessity always unexplorable.

Ignatius assigns a full week for the Passion, to be entered upon "with a great effort," and to be continued with the whole-hearted cooperation with grace which we have described. When the week is finished he wants his exercitant to take another whole day, during which to live through the details of the story, taking "the first half." Then yet another extra day, during which he will soak his mind and heart in "the second half" of the Passion. Not yet is he satisfied. Could the exercitant manage to spare one more extra day which will give him opportunity to view the Passion "as a whole?" From all this it is abundantly clear what high store he set on the third week.

The Passion is a divine romance. The great Lover is omnipotent and here we find Him almost taxing the powers of His omnipotence in order to remove every vestige of possible doubt regarding the sincerity of His love. If the Passion does not convince me of this, there is no more that an omnipotent Lover can do to bring conviction. The Passion is a wonderful love story, the most thrilling, the most amazing ever written. It is written in red, the red ink of the Precious Blood. It is written in a language intelligible to every true lover, the language of self-sacrifice. St. Paul supplies the title when he says that Christ "loved me and gave himself up for me." [1] St. John puts it in similar fashion: "God so loved the world that he gave his only-begotten Son." [2]

Throughout this week St. Ignatius would have his exercitant all the while store deep in his mind two profound truths. First, the sufferer is God! That man in the embrace of Judas the traitor is God, the Second Person of the Blessed Trinity. God lies prostrate under the olive trees in Gethsemani and sweats blood. I kneel in the barrack yard of Pilate's palace and see a poor prisoner who has just collapsed at the base of the pillar—He is God, enduring an inhuman scourging at the hands of His creatures. God is dragged out of that pool of blood, flung into a sitting position, jeered at, derided, blindfolded, and spat upon. It may well be maintained that no gesture is more expressive of contempt than to spit on a person. Men dared to stand in front of God and spit on His face.

God stumbled, more dead than alive, through the narrow, crowded streets, over the rocky roads, bent low under the weight of a cross. God was nailed to that cross, hung there for hours in exquisite agony, refused to come down when His enemies defied Him to do so, and remained there suffering till finally death came to give Him relief. For a man with the deep faith of Ignatius this one fact about the Person suffering would, of itself alone, provide material for inexhaustible meditation.

If we were to judge by mere external appearances, which of us would have suspected that He was God? "The divinity hides itself," writes Ignatius, and it is his second "key" as he proceeds to open for us the treasure-house of the Passion. God suffers, but He is a "hidden God." How a single gesture of impatience, however excusable, would have marred the beauty of this drama! As God stands before Pilate, His back "ploughed up" by the fearful scourging, His head crowned with thorns, His eyes almost shut, weighed down by blood and spittle, He alone, thus humiliated, is still fully self-possessed. The mob yelling around Him, the enraged High Priests, the vacillating Pilate—all these are taut, "on edge," clearly

they have lost control of themselves badly. But not so this
man. Victim of their insane hatred, He stands there above
them, the one person who maintains perfect tranquillity
of conduct, an index to the abiding peace in His soul.
Had they only eyes to see, the very bearing of this man
must have shown them that He was God. No mere man
could behave as He is behaving. But their eyes are held;
"the divinity hides itself."

The sufferer employs His divine power for one purpose only—in order to enable Him to suffer the more. To
some contemplative soul He revealed that He must have
died during the scourging at the pillar had He not supported His life by a miracle. This seems highly credible.
It is further evidence of the eagerness with which He
stretched out arms of welcome to suffering, for love invariably translates itself into acts of self-sacrifice.

The love in the human heart is limited in quantity, and
the greater the number upon whom it is spread the less
there will be for each individual. Thus St. Paul reminds
us that an unmarried person is often capable of loving
God more than one who is married. In the latter case,
in the apostle's word, there is more likelihood of the love
being "divided." Of course this is not true universally.
But God's love is different. The Sacred Heart reminded
St. Margaret Mary that no matter how many come to
Him in response to His appeal for love, there will always
be a superfluity, since in this case the love is infinite.

Hence St. Paul can say with truth that Christ loved
"me" and "gave himself up for 'me.'" [3] There is an
exquisite scene described by the evangelist where our
Lord encounters a great number of sick. They have been

placed along His route in the town during the cool of the evening. How does He treat them? Give them a general blessing and dismiss them? Not so. He lays His hands on each single individual, and He heals them all. There is the personal touch. Each one of these poor sufferers has a special place in His love.

The same personal touch shines forth in His love as manifested throughout His Sacred Passion. Ignatius has not missed it. He would not have me regard the Passion as a proof of our Lord's love for the millions of men who people the earth, at least not as that only. It is an act of personal love, shown for me individually by the God-man. *I* am worth all this. To win *me* completely to Him, He is prepared to endure it. Were my soul the only one to be redeemed He would joyfully pay the same price. The Preface of the Mass of the Sacred Heart reminds us of the "torrents of mercy and of grace," stored up in this "treasure house." Like water piled up and pressing against a dam, this love seeks to break down every barrier and spread its healing everywhere, transforming every soul, fructifying each, communicating to each a sharing in the new life of grace won by the Passion.

The petition on the lips and in the heart of the exercitant, as he strives to live the Passion over again, is for "sympathy" with Christ. Ignatius would have the weight of all this suffering lean upon him, crush him almost. He must suffer with our Lord—feeling some of His physical pain, oppressed with that haunting sense of loneliness, of failure, of disappointment and frustration, which are easy to detect in Christ as He moves from event to event in the drama. "Could you not, then, watch one hour *with me?*" [4] So the earnest soul begs for sorrow with Christ full of sorrow, tears even, and bitterness, in union with Christ who deigns to endure such things, as "for my sins He goes to His Sacred Passion."

Ignatius attaches much importance to feelings. Several times throughout the Exercises we are told to beg for feelings in harmony with the subject matter of our prayer. True, he recognizes that they are not an infallible criterion of the worth of our prayer, but they can be a powerful help, and the saint wants to employ every possible means to win his man, a creature of intellect, and will, and imagination, and emotions—"all that there is in man"—to the divine service and praise. As we noticed on another page, he employs the same verb as St. Paul, *sentire.* The soul may not give up effort when feelings of sweetness are withdrawn, but it should use them to the full as long as they last, and there is nothing wrong in hoping they may return and, as here, in begging them from God, should He see fit to grant them.

Omniscience could devise no more effective means of repairing the havoc done by sin than voluntary suffering. Infinite love could find no more sure way of winning men's hearts than to endure sufferings. Hence the enamored soul of Ignatius experiences a craving to suffer with Christ, and bids his exercitant to beg for a like craving. Not only "with" Him must the soul suffer, but "in" Him. Sanctified suffering is an extension of the Passion and an application of its infinite merits to needy souls. Our sufferings, accepted in a Christian spirit, are like tributaries to the vast ocean. The ocean of His sufferings and our contributions both flow along together, cleansing and sanctifying as they flow.

Thus does a man fill up in his flesh what is wanting to the sufferings of Christ, for His Body which is the Church. "In His capacity of direct and invisible Ruler of the Church," writes Pope Pius XII in *Mystici Corporis*, "Our Savior wants to be helped by the members of His Mystical Body in carrying out the work of redemption. This is not due to any insufficiency in Him, but rather because He has so ordained it for the greater glory of His immaculate Bride. Dying on the cross, He bestowed upon His Church the boundless treasure of the redemption without any cooperation on her part; but in the distribution of that treasure. He not only shares this work of sanctification with His spotless Bride, but wills it to arise in a certain manner out of her labor.

"This is truly a tremendous mystery, upon which we can never meditate enough—that the salvation of many souls depends upon *the prayers and voluntary mortifications* offered for that intention by the members of the Mystical Body of Jesus Christ, and upon the cooperation which pastors and faithful, and especially parents, must afford to our divine Savior."

The Passion is a love story, the most amazing love story ever written. And the most amazing feature of the story is that, unlike most others which we have read, this one is all true. It is not written merely to entertain or interest us, merely to exhibit the virtues of the hero who is its center and move us to admiration and perhaps to imitation. It is written because it is the sheer, unadorned, unadulterated truth. The effects of the Passion are still being produced. Christ is still suffering in the members of His Mystical Body. Through these the fruits of the Passion are being applied still, to this day and to this hour, to souls. The grain of wheat dies only that it may bring forth abundant fruit.

The work of our redemption is being exercised still; "Jesus Christ is the same, yesterday and today, yes, and forever." [5]

XIX

THE SERENITY OF CHRIST

THE triumph of the wicked galls us even to read about. The flagrant and brazen injustices against the Church, described for instance in *The Red Book*, must stir up our anger and we cannot but wish we had it in our power to bring those guilty to justice. Now in the Passion our Lord was absolutely at the mercy of the worst criminals in history, utterly corrupt and unscrupulous and determined on His death. At any moment He could have thrown them into panic by revealing His divinity—but He refrained from doing so. "The divinity remains hid." At any moment He could have torn the mask of hypocrisy from their faces, He could have frozen their hearts with terror by a miraculous vindication of His rights, He could have summoned twelve legions of angels to scatter confusion in their ranks. To our thinking it would have been a deed well done, but the Savior judges differently. In our righteous indignation we want Him to call down fire from heaven to chastize them and annihilate them, but our impetuous zeal He meets with but scant approval.

This perfect self-mastery, this serenity of Christ under what should ordinarily be maddeningly provoking, what is its secret? You know that if a person is preoccupied with an important task he can easily forget about the common conventions of life. A man whose interest is gripped by a book may fail to keep an appointment. A soldier in the heat of the fight may not advert to the fact that he has received a serious wound. A boxer or football player, immersed in the game, passes off lightly a hurt which at another time would call forth loud complaints.

Throughout the Passion the mind and heart of our Lord are set on a task so vast that it seems to dwarf even His terrible sufferings. We do not for a moment suggest that this task had the effect of a drug rendering Him actually irresponsive to His pains. He is indeed vividly conscious of every single torture, mental and physical, but the memory of the object for which they are endured also persists the whole time. For His Passion is a mighty exorcism by which Satan is being expelled from the souls of men. Thus the mind of Christ is fixed on an object even higher and greater than His sufferings. To the divine Exorcist, enamored of the souls of men, the cost of the exorcism is little in view of the liberty soon to be restored to the sons of God.

There is a further explanation of the serenity of Christ. All through His life our blessed Lord saw the face of His heavenly Father in the full splendor and beauty of the Beatific Vision, saw Him with a more penetrating clarity than that with which we see each other here on earth, looked continually into the infinite love and lovableness that is God. So flooded with light was the mind of Christ, so transported with love was the heart of Christ, that any suffering was endurable, more, was welcomed by Him, if it could contribute to atoning for crimes committed against God who is infinitely good and infinitely perfect.

That is why "Jesus kept silence" [1] when we would

think He should have defended Himself with a showing of energy. That is why "when He was reviled, [He] did not revile." [2] That is why He was "led as a sheep to the slaughter" [3] and opened not His mouth, "becoming obedient to death, even to death on a cross," [4] because by such obedience He could best give expression to the love that consumed Him, love of the Father, love of us.

It is clear that St. Ignatius saw life in this way. It is certain that he ardently wished the same mentality to develop in his exercitant. The soul he has undertaken to guide will not indeed be favored with the Beatific Vision in this life, else it must die of love. But he hopes that it will become anchored in God. He expects that God will become the lodestar of his exercitant's life, so that he will recognize God as the one enduring, abiding Reality in a world of change. In God's sight he must prostrate himself making to God the unqualified offering of himself. Christ our Lord saw the face of His Father in the beauty of the Beatific Vision. The soul lives by faith, sees Him, though it be through a glass darkly and not yet face to face; but even that obscure vision convinces that provided His will be done nothing else matters much or at all.

This immovable persuasion would seem to be what St. Paul was thinking of when he wrote to the Philippians: "Have this mind in you which was also in Christ Jesus." [5] Language of this sort is unintelligible to those who either are ignorant of God or have only the crudest notion of His unutterable perfections. But the soul that begins to sense the Passion swiftly goes on to drink from a fountain that is inexhaustible deep draughts of that peace of God surpassing all understanding. To that soul a new perspective is given, in the light of which it sees with a clarity baffling its powers to express, that one only matters—God; one design only is of importance—the perfect, loving, unremitting effort to accept and obey His rulings in all things. That is the mentality that is in a state of receptivity, ready to absorb into itself the serenity of Christ and radiate it and communicate it to others.

One of our greatest trials is our dependence on the whims of others. Our Lord voluntarily submitted to that trial. He was a mere pawn in the game played by His iniquitous judges. The secret of His unruffled serenity we are trying to discover in order to rule ourselves by its light when all that is natural in us wants to cry out against injustice, misrepresentation, misunderstanding, more especially when these are deliberate. To learn the hard lesson of silent, patient endurance, to adopt this as a fixed principle, relying on the strength of His grace and the inspiration of His example in the Passion, is to experience in ourselves the beneficent effects of the serenity of Christ.

Go back in thought ten or twelve years. How agitated you then were over some accident, over some act of unkindness, some harsh word, a sum of money you had lost, sickness, or an operation! In retrospect how insignificant it all seems now, and yet at the time you thought it meant the end of the world. Such things disturb our mental equilibrium in the measure in which we are not anchored in God.

How is the exercitant going to react to such foolish wisdom? Ignatius never fails to remind him to "apply all this to himself." There are those who regard this wisdom as folly, and there are those to whom this foolishness is true wisdom. There are "fools for Christ," [6] and those who, "professing to be wise, . . . have become fools." [7]

The different reactions to the cross may be summed up under three headings. One class rejects the whole doctrine of the value of suffering. Suffering of whatsoever kind, mental or physical, is an unmitigated misfortune with nothing to recommend it. This class logically spends life in trying to shirk the cross. The second class accepts Christ, but in spite of the cross. For them too the cross is a stumbling block. They would wish for a Christ without it, but since that is not possible, they grudgingly accept Him as they find Him. But the saints are those who love Him precisely because of the cross. They have learned its secrets—some of its secrets—and what they have learned has quickened in them the yearning to explore and discover further.

A worthy son of Ignatius, a man steeped in the spirit of the Exercises, sings the praises of suffering in the following eloquent passage: "By means of sufferings the soul arrives at great holiness and at a close imitation of the crucified Son of God. Thence arise true peace of soul (the serenity of Christ) and continual prayer. Thence a genuine union of the soul with God, the perpetual presence of God, and purity and stainlessness of soul. Thence humble familiarity with God. Thence perfect charity, the love of God and of one's neighbor. Thence the seraphim's crown of glory. Thence great spiritual treasures and riches which God is wont to bestow in abundance on souls in trials, and favors and heavenly secrets which God discloses to them, favors such and so great as are known only to God and to the soul that receives them; for such and so great are they that they may be tasted but not told, for they take place between God and the soul alone. . . .

"O sweetest Jesus, love of my soul, center of my heart! How is it that I do not desire with stronger desire to endure pains and tortures for love of Thee, when Thou, my God, hast suffered so many for me? O sufferings, how I hope that you will come to me and make your stay within my heart, for in you I find my repose, and I will go to the heart of my crucified Jesus, there to dwell in it with you. O torments, how is it that you do not come upon me who await you with open arms, that with you I may rejoice with my Jesus in torture? O dishonor, why do you forget me who never forget you, because I love you so much in order that I may behold myself debased by you and humbled with Jesus? O ignominious deaths, why do you not come upon me in thousands when I desire so much and wish so continually to sacrifice myself to my Jesus?

"Come then, every sort of trial in this world, for this is my delight, to suffer for Jesus. This is my joy, to follow my Savior, and to find my consolation and my consoler on the cross. This is my pleasure, this my delight, to live with Jesus, to walk with Jesus, to converse with Jesus; to suffer with and for Him, this is my treasure." (From St. Alphonsus Rodriguez.)

One feels inclined to transcribe more, but enough has been said to show the attitude of the saints towards the cross and suffering, and to encourage us, who in our frailty follow them afar off, towards a keener understanding of their excesses. This is the price of the serenity of Christ and they are the first to assure us that it is purchased cheap. This is not to have Christ in spite of the cross, still less to reject the cross. It is eager acceptance.

It is the attitude of Christ Himself who, on the night of the Last Supper, "knowing all that was to come upon him," [8] went forth to find the cross, and having found, to embrace it. "It was not so much the death or Passion of Christ which paid the price of our sin, as the love with which He endured it."

XX

TEARS OF CHRIST

THE missal has a prayer for the gift of tears. "Almighty and most loving God, who to quench the thirst of Thy people didst draw a fountain of living water out of a rock; draw from our stony hearts tears of compunction, that we may be able to mourn for our sins and win forgiveness for them from Thy mercy. . . . Look down, O Lord, in mercy on the offerings which we make to Thy majesty for our sins, and draw from our eyes such streams of tears as may quench the burning flames which we deserve. . . . Mercifully pour into our hearts, O Lord God, the grace of the Holy Ghost, which by sighs and tears may make us wash away the stains of our sins, and obtain for us, by Thy bounty, the pardon which we desire. Through our Lord, Jesus Christ."

In the Exercises too, notably in the third week, St. Ignatius bids us pray for tears of sorrow in union with the tears shed by the suffering Christ. So frequently and so copiously did he himself weep—while saying Mass particularly, and reciting the Office—that he was in grave danger of injuring his sight. Divine consolations were so abundant that sometimes it would take him hours to get through the Holy Sacrifice.

So strong men can weep and be convinced that in their tears there is nothing derogatory to their manhood. There is "a time to weep and a time to laugh." [1] Our Lord Himself shed tears; "with a loud cry and tears, [He] offered up prayers and supplications . . . and was heard because of his reverent submission." [2] The third week would seem to be appropriate for a prayerful study of the tears of our Lord, even though that study will take us a little outside the realm of the Passion story.

There are only two explicit references to precise occasions on which Jesus wept. One of these was at the grave of His friend Lazarus. The other was when He rode over Olivet and looked down on Jerusalem lying at His feet. "And when he drew near and saw the city, he wept over it." [3] The text quoted from St. Paul seems to imply that there were other times, but of these there is no concise record.

Why did He weep? His tears were caused in both the cases listed by compassion. The sight of Martha and Mary, so forlorn, so desolate, awakened at once a response in the Sacred Heart. We remember that "Jesus loved Martha and her sister Mary, and Lazarus." [4] This was a family in Bethany where He could always be sure of a welcome. He was glad to go there when wearied by the heckling and hair-splitting arguments of scribes and pharisees persistently trying to catch Him in His speech. There was deep distress in Bethany today, and because Jesus loved, He wept on seeing it.

For the same reason He wept over Jerusalem. This was "his own town." [5] To this people He had given of His best; for them He was about to die; He had warned and argued and wrought miracles before them and all to no purpose. They would fail Him and He knew it. And they are so pitifully sure of themselves, so blind to their own misery, so insensible to what they are losing, a volatile, irresponsible people, ignorant of the day of their visitation. He knew what He wanted to give to them, what He would have them to be, but they cared not at all "and Jesus wept." [6]

When men cease to believe in this sympathy of Christ they become hardened and embittered by trials. Without Him life is empty, a blind alley, an insoluble riddle, and they see no point in going on, enduring aimlessly. In a futile attempt to avenge themselves on the world, and on Him, they put an end to their own lives. It seems the easy way out. It looks like a simple solution, perhaps the only solution, and without the knowledge of Christ's sympathy and the support it gives, one can understand why men accept it as such. "If with this life only in view we have had hope in Christ," if He be a mere man who dreamed dreams, then indeed "we are of all men the most to be pitied." [7] Why remain "here, where men sit and hear each other groan?"

But in the Christian heart there is a bright ray of sunshine all the time. Even though the poor sufferer may wonder why he is called upon to suffer, and especially to suffer in this precise way, even though the temptation be strong to break out into complaints, and even though in moments of peculiar agony he may yield to its urge, still there abides this firm conviction: "Christ loves me; Christ has sympathy with me; He sees and understands my struggle; for reasons which I shall one day know He permits this suffering; meanwhile I am certain that the explanation lies in the fact that He loves me." "Jesus Christ is the same, yesterday and today, yes, and forever" [8] and He has not changed since the days when He wept over Jerusalem; the compassion shown in the house at Bethany is as deep and sincere now as it was then. This the Christian's faith tells him. This conviction penetrates into the innermost recesses of his soul, a light in dark places, a tower of strength, a fountain of living water springing up to life everlasting.

Suffering accepted in this spirit saves the sufferer from the canker of self-pity. So far from becoming preoccupied with himself, he tends rather to go out in compassion toward others. All through the Passion our Lord, despite His own excruciating agony, was all the time thinking how He could help others. One time it was Judas; another time it was Peter, or the weeping women, or the men who nailed Him to the cross, or the repentant thief, or the Mother who stood by the cross. Whoever He concerns Himself about, of this we may be certain—it is a foregone conclusion—that it is never Himself.

What else would have caused the tears shed by our Lord? Surely there were tears of deep compunction, a result of the vision that haunted His mind of the nature of sin. Remember that He always saw the face of His Father in heaven. He knew therefore the infinite beauty of the Godhead. "If a soul," writes St. John of the Cross, "had but one single glimpse of the grandeur and beauty of God, it would not only desire to die once in order to behold Him. It would joyfully endure a thousand most bitter deaths to behold Him even for a moment, and having seen Him, would suffer as many deaths *again* in order to behold Him for another moment."

We grieve, and often express indignation, if a son or daughter is lacking in the respect or affection due to a parent to whom they owe everything—to a father who

has worked hard and patiently to provide a good education for that child, to a mother who has struggled with
poverty and hunger and left nothing undone to train that
child by word and example. We are indignant at the
callousness of the child; such parents deserve better.

"Who can detect failings?" [9] Only One can understand what God is, against whom sin is a deliberate insult.
If every human being became a saint, if every one of us
practiced heroic virtue sustained all through our lives,
even then the race would be hopelessly in debt. Nothing
that all finite beings combined could do would be sufficient to atone for a single sin committed against the infinitely perfect God. What then is to be said of a race
that multiplies its crimes every day, every hour? "Hear,
O ye heavens, and give ear O earth, for the Lord God
hath spoken: 'I have brought up children and exalted
them, but they have despised me.' " [10]

It is indeed reasonable to suppose that the eyes of Christ
were often wet with tears, especially during the Passion,
when He saw on the one hand the ineffable sanctity of
the Father, and on the other the outrages done against
Him by men.

Tears of compunction are called for in our day and
in our hour. Every thinking person must recognize the
need to make reparation to God's majesty, not only for
our own sins, but for crimes devastating the world—
leading it, wrote Belloc, into a new paganism which
"foolishly expecting satisfaction, will fall, before it knows
where it is, into Satanism!"

That was twenty-five years ago, perhaps not quite that
much. Is not the proved truth of his words argument
for tears of compunction?

Lastly Jesus wept, we may suppose, from a mere sense of anguish. He was like us in everything except sin. Sorrow crushed Him and expressed itself in Him, as in ourselves, by tears. His soul was exquisitely sensitive to pain and in times of mental depression, as in times of physical suffering, we may believe that He sought relief in weeping. Did He weep thus in Gethsemani, or on the cross? "With a loud cry and tears [He] offered up prayers and supplications ... and was heard because of his reverent submission." [11] Tears are no sign of weakness, still less do they show any reluctance on His part to suffer. He sheds them because, being a real man, He reacted to pain and sorrow as other men do. Further His tears are our instruction, our consolation.

It is fitting that an exile should shed tears, and we are away from home "mourning and weeping in this valley of tears"—tears of compassion, tears of compunction, tears called forth by excess of grief. But even on the land of exile the sun shines too, and high up above the cries of sorrow the promise rings out, like the sweet notes of a silver trumpet. "God will wipe away every tear from their eyes. And death shall be no more; neither shall there be mourning, nor crying, nor pain any more, for the former things have passed away. And he who was sitting on the throne said: 'Behold, I make all things new.' " [12]

XXI

LIGHT AND SHADE

A book or instruction on prayer has value in the measure in which it is the outcome of personal experience. St. Teresa often speaks about "a certain nun" whom she knows, whose prayer she describes, and naïvely expects us not to suspect that nun's identity. That St. John of the Cross and St. Alphonsus Rodriguez learned their sublime doctrine on prayer from their own intimate relations with God is evident on every page they wrote. The same is true of the Exercises. Ignatius, most reticent indeed about the secrets of his interior life, confessed that if the truths of the faith were all lost he would still adhere to them with absolute devotion as a result of what had been vouchsafed to him in Manresa.

Teresa, Ignatius, John of the Cross, and Alphonsus— there you have a galaxy of luminaries who have told us, each in his own way, of what each personally experienced in the soul's ascent to God.

We can imagine no more fascinating study than a detailed comparison of these four authorities on the science of prayer. The unanimity which would evolve in their teaching concerning fundamentals would offset the diversity to be found in the different development of each under the action of "one and the same Spirit." [1] It is probably true that no two souls pray in precisely the same way, just as no two children employ the exact same language in talking to their father. Certain elements are identical but there is a refreshing variety too. "There is one glory of the sun, and another glory of the moon, and another of the stars; for star differs from star in glory." [2]

For the moment however we have to limit ourselves to a page in the Exercises where Ignatius, eager as always to help us to pray, gives us some principles gleaned from experience, and sifted and tested thoroughly before he formulated them into trustworthy rules.

How are we to understand whether it is God's grace or the Evil Spirit who is acting in our soul? If a man is living habitually in grave sin, answers Ignatius, if he makes light of sin and easily falls from mortal sin to mortal sin, grace will affect him in a manner diametrically different from Satan. The enemy will lure such a one on by holding out vain promises of happiness in further sin, firing his imagination and stirring up his desires, persuading him that the sensual pleasures he craves for will completely satisfy his longings. This lie the tempter continues to perpetrate, even though his poor victim may have already learned many times, by bitter experience, that to yield does no more than lead to a feeling of futility, and goad the soul recklessly to further excesses.

But the good spirit offers to such a soul no soft assurances. On the contrary it is proper to the grace of God to cause remorse and wholesome anxiety by which the soul may be aroused to realize its ingratitude and its peril and draw back while there is yet time.

Now take a man who sincerely strives to lead a good life. He is sober, pure, honest, faithful to prayer. On him the two spirits will act differently. In this case the enemy will try to fill him with dread, discouragement, scruples, in order to turn him back, whereas the good spirit will tend to console such a soul, giving it a deep sense of peace, helping it to rid itself of obstacles, sending light to the mind, all with the object of urging it forward to greater love of God and neighbor.

By "consolation" St. Ignatius tells us he means "any movement in the soul by which the soul begins to be inflamed with love of God and feels it can never again love anything or anyone except in Him. This love may express itself in tears—of sorrow for one's sins or of grief for the sufferings of our Lord, or these tears may be caused by any subject directly relating to the service and praise of God. Consolation is, further, every increase in Faith, Hope and Charity, all spiritual joy which attracts the soul to the things of heaven ... rendering it full of tranquillity in its Creator and Lord."

"O my Jesus," exclaims St. Teresa, "what a sight it is to see a soul that has attained as far as this, and has fallen into sin, when Thou of Thy Mercy stretchest forth Thy hand to it again and raisest it up! How conscious it becomes of the multitude of Thy wonders and mercies, and of its own wretchedness! Now indeed is it consumed with shame when it acknowledges Thy wonders. Now it dares not lift its eyes to Thee. Now it raises them only to acknowledge what it owes Thee. Now it devoutly beseeches the Queen of heaven to propitiate Thee. Now it invokes the saints who likewise fell after Thou hadst called them, that they may aid it. Now it feels all Thou givest to be bounty indeed, for it knows itself to be unworthy even of the ground it treads upon. It has recourse to the Sacraments and a lively faith is implanted in it when it sees what virtues God has placed in them. . . . I cannot think why my heart does not break as I write this, wicked that I am."

Desolation is everything contrary to what Ignatius has described as consolation—darkness in the soul, restless agitation, temptation to despair, so that the soul finds itself full of sorrow and depression and inclined to doubt God's mercy. In such a time of trial it would be fatal to make any change in one's relations with God—the soul at all costs must hold on to its resolutions; more, not only should it persevere in its accustomed prayer but should lengthen it, not only should it not abandon its practice of penance but should force itself to insist all the more. And let the soul be full of courage. This period of desolation is only a trial permitted by God. He wants the soul to prove its love, and He assures it that it can conquer because His grace will never be wanting to it. When this desolation has effected what God intends it to do, it will disappear and consolation will return, more especially if the soul will persevere for the time all the more faithfully in prayer and penance.

We lose divine consolations and fall into desolation, first, through our own fault. We grow weary of the struggle, we tone down our resolutions, we turn to creatures and try to find our happiness in them. God will never force His gifts upon us. Any truce with sin or imperfection, any effort to substitute the comfort afforded by creatures for the love and praise of the Creator, and the soul dries up, losing its relish for the things of God. St. John of the Cross covers many a page in expanding what St. Ignatius states so tersely here. He breaks out into bitter laments that so many souls find the upward

Godward journey too hard at this juncture, turn back, and walk with Him no more.

These spiritual crises are also meant to test and prove the solidity of our devotion to God. How far are we prepared to go in our loyal service when we find ourselves suddenly deprived of all sensible satisfaction? "I fed you with milk, not with solid food," wrote St. Paul, "for you were not yet ready for it. Nor are you now ready for it, for you are still carnal." [3] Peter was very loud, and very sincere, in his professions of loyalty at the Last Supper. It was in the hour of trial that the test came and we know, alas, how he fared.

Lastly desolation and dryness convince us that the former sweetness we had is, pure and simple, a free gift of God. We cannot have it when we like and God withdraws it, through no fault of ours, in order to save us from pride and vainglory.

In consolation it is good to remember that desolation will return. Now is the time to observe how inconstant the soul can be under the test; let it now forestall the tendency to despondency which may follow. Let it bring home to itself the realization of its own weakness, how listless it can become and how cowardly under the onslaught of desolation. Where would it end did a merciful God not hasten at such a time to raise it up by His grace? On the other hand, when in desolation, the soul should take heart, placing all its trust in God, remaining quite certain that through His grace it can overcome every attack of Satan.

For the exercitant must never forget that the devil is a coward. He is like a woman who quarrels with a man. If the man lets her see that he is afraid, if he flees from her fury, her boldness will increase. But let him face her calmly and resolutely and very soon her courage fizzles out. In like manner the devil, on discovering that the person he strives to lead astray opposes him firmly and does the exact opposite of what he suggests, slinks away from him, utterly routed. It is only when the person begins to show dread, only when he lets the Evil One see he is losing heart under stress of trial, that the coward is emboldened to press his advantage. There is now no beast on the face of the earth more savage and more obstinate than he in pursuing his wicked design. You know how a false lover behaves, tempting the woman who infatuates him, and warning her above all else to keep secret from her father or husband the advances he makes. He knows well that his game is up if she tells. Satan is like that. He is the spirit of darkness and he is filled with anger if the soul reveals to a prudent confessor or spiritual director the trials it is undergoing.

A general who wants to capture a fort or a city will walk around and examine till he finds what spot in the defense is weakest. (St. Ignatius wrote four hundred years ago!) Having discovered it, he will bring all his strength to bear on that one spot in order to effect a breach. So does Satan study the soul, so does he observe the weakness inherent in each person's character and plan accordingly. Having found it he will leave nothing undone to create occasions which tempt the soul in that precise spot. It will therefore be the soul's special task to be particularly on its guard wherever it foresees that it is most likely to be attacked.

Spiritual joy is the gift of God who can at any moment sweep away the disturbances caused by Satan and fill the soul with happiness. This He can do, and only He can do it, by entering into the soul as into His own house, wonderfully drawing the soul to love Him—even though the soul may not have done anything itself to bring about this happy state of things. St. John of the Cross was locked up in prison for ten months and had much to suffer. He afterwards declared that in that ten months he experienced such inundations of heavenly consolation that, for a single moment of them, a whole lifetime of the sufferings would be a small price to pay.

If you can put your finger on something which causes this feeling of exaltation, you must know that it may be due either to God's action or to the action of the Evil One. Satan can transform himself into an angel of light. He can collaborate with the soul in its spiritual strivings, even suggesting good thoughts and resolutions, but all with the object of establishing the soul in a false security. That is why our thoughts and desires need to be carefully scrutinized. How do they start? How do they progress? To what do they finally lead? If it is evident that an idea or suggestion is good under all three headings, then clearly it is from God.

When you detect the "serpent's tail"—the sinful, or less perfect, end to which the tempter was leading you —you might with much profit look back and study the entire technique he employed. You should be able to recognize the point at which he began to inject his poison, serving up specious reasons to persuade you, for example, that you were aiming too high, that you were presumptuous to make such a resolution, that God does not expect so much from such as you, that there is danger of pride or hypocrisy in what you proposed to yourself.

A soul that loves God and is fervent in His service can recognize Satan's tactics by the fact that they run counter to the state of the soul. The Evil Spirit acts on such a fervent soul like water falling on a rock. But God acts on it peacefully; His action is compared to water falling on a sponge. If the soul is worldly, if it is given to sin, Satan now whispers softly that all is well, but divine grace speaks words of stern warning. A tepid soul can know what is of God and what is of Satan because here the voice of God is like water on a rock and the soothing accents of Satan are like water falling on the sponge.

Divine consolation should be carefully distinguished from the period immediately following it. Often after God's action has ceased the soul will still feel itself in a state of great sweetness and fervor. It could easily happen that at this time the soul might make promises or form projects, under the persuasion that it was being moved to do so by God. Such resolutions or projects should by no means be readily acted upon. They require expert examination if serious illusion is to be avoided.

This chapter is practically a translation of what Ignatius wrote four hundred years ago. We can hardly expect the style to be modern or some of his similes to be still apt. But there is here the wisdom which sitteth by God's throne which Solomon prayed might be given to him. Truth does not change and divine wisdom is eternal. A prayerful study of the doctrine of Ignatius will reveal a depth of wisdom and an exalted truth in which is latent the solution to many of our problems.

XXII

REJOICE ALWAYS

THE sight of suffering moves us to sympathy instinctively. Even a complete stranger might enter into another's sorrow. If I see a man crushed under the wheel of a car and writhing in agony there is a spontaneous urge in me to try to set him free. If I visit a hospital and come upon a poor patient disfigured with lupus or cancer the sight calls forth—even if I do not want it—a feeling of pity, and if there be some service I can do for that suffering man or woman I gladly avail myself of the opportunity as providing me with material to prove the reality of my affection.

But the joys of another evoke no such immediate response. I am only mildly interested to learn that John Smith has come into a huge fortune or to hear that Jim Jones is found innocent of the crime charged against him. If in such a case I show signs of great delight people will conclude that John or Jim are personal friends of mine. That is why it is perhaps a greater proof of love to rejoice in the joy of another than to grieve with him when he is pressed down under a weight of sorrow.

The joy of our divine Lord in His Resurrection is the greatest created joy that ever was. It is all the more intense because it was preceded by so much suffering. A woman in labor has sorrow, but when the child is brought

forth her joy is so deep that she forgets all about what
she had to endure. "And you therefore have sorrow now;
but I will see you again and your heart shall rejoice, and
your joy no one shall take from you." [1]

This is the keynote of the fourth week of St. Ignatius'
Exercises. The soul enamored of Jesus Christ has been
urged to plunge with Him into the sea of His sorrows.
But it is now invited to drink of the torrents of joy that
inundate His soul. Because it has been captivated by love
it finds itself in an ecstasy of happiness on beholding His
triumph over sin and death. The apostle's words resound
like a refrain in the heart: "Christ, having risen from the
dead, dies now no more; death shall no longer have dominion over him." [2]

We are told to rejoice not only because the One we
love is forever immune from the possibility of further
suffering, not only because He stands in the Resurrection
in the blaze of light that bespeaks His victory, but also
because His Resurrection is the pledge and model of our
own. The work of the Passion, the mighty exorcism, was
the destruction of sin, something negative. The object of
the Resurrection is positive, the infusing of new life. "As
Christ has risen from the dead through the glory of the
Father, so we also may walk in newness of life." [3]

The spiritual life means *living habitually* under the influence of a keen realization of the fact of Christ. He is
my greater self, and I am fashioned to be like Him. No
mere submission to an external rule, be it ever so exact,
will effect this fashioning. He must increase; I must de-
crease. I am to be an extension of His life. It must be
reproduced in me, and not the Passion only but the glory,
and that glory begins even here in the land of exile with

the infusion and growth of grace in my soul. "Now we
are the children of God, and it has not yet appeared what
we shall be." [4] Intellectual delights are the keenest of all,
yet in this life they are mere spray from the infinite ocean
to be explored hereafter. Grace in the soul is the germ
of immortal life.

These are some of the reasons for the first note set by
Ignatius at the opening of the fourth week. "Rejoice in
the Lord always; again I say, rejoice!" [5]

In this place too he would have us consider how the
Risen Christ exercises the office of consoler. With the
eye of faith we can watch His triumphant entry into
Limbo and witness the transports of joy of the souls imprisoned there. Adam and Eve see their fault now fully
expiated. We might well suppose that they anticipated
the hymn of gladness which would later rise up in the
heart of the Church: "O felix culpa! Happy fault of ours
indeed which merited a Redeemer such as Christ!" Abel,
whose death was a symbol of the death of the Savior,
exults that what was prefigured in him is perfectly fulfilled in our Lord. The first Abraham to whom were made
"many and great promises" is gladdened to know that
they are realized now. The prophets Isaias and David and
Daniel are brought face to face with Him, the obscure
vision of whom ravished their hearts. St. Joseph sees his
much-loved foster-Son glorified. The Baptist recognizes
once more the Lamb of God who has taken away the sin
of the world. The Good Thief who called Him "Lord,"
discerning even in the humiliation of the Passion that this
man was no common criminal, notes the joyous contrast
between the bleeding, thorn-crowned sufferer and the
Risen Christ whose eyes and countenance are today

flooded with divine light, whose head today is encircled in a halo of glory. "Worthy art thou, O Lord our God, to receive glory, and honor, and power." [6] "Worthy is the Lamb who was slain to receive power, and divinity, and wisdom, and strength, and honor, and glory, and blessing. . . . To the Lamb blessing, and honor and glory and dominion, forever and ever." [7]

The same "office of consoler" He exercises among those friends of His who had shared with Him the griefs of the Passion. During the forty days He comes constantly into their midst, at times most unexpectedly, and their hearts burn within them and the peace of God surpassing all understanding possesses their souls.

XXIII

DIVINE VISITATIONS

WE have no difficulty in believing with St. Ignatius that before any other our Lord came to His Mother. Perhaps a reason why we have no record of this coming is that it would have been known to our Lady alone, and what passed between them was too sacred, too precious an ointment for its fragrance to be shared with others, too personal and intimate an experience; so sublime that Mary alone could grasp the meaning of the secret words spoken and she alone could endure the awful nearness of divinity therein revealed. We know that the prophet could only say in stammering speech what God had shown him of Himself. We know that St. Paul despairs of communicating to us the depth and beauty of the hidden words he heard when "caught up to the third heaven." [1] Small wonder then if our Lady preserves silence concerning what took place on that first Easter morning when He came to her to exercise the office of consoler.

But with Ignatius we can kneel in lowly reverence between them. Did Mary rush forward to embrace Him? One scarcely thinks so. One would incline to say that her joy on seeing this transformation was so overpowering that she was just able to endure it. She remained there on her knees, rooted to the spot; her eyes riveted upon Him; any further inundation of this ecstatic happiness and she must have swooned and died. In the whole history of the human race can there ever have been joy to compare with what is found today in the Sacred Heart of Christ and the Immaculate Heart of Mary?

From Mary the sinless He goes to Mary who had lived in the city "a sinner." Since that day on which He had won her, Magdalene has been the inseparable companion and intimate of His Mother. He stands before her in the garden and draws her story from her. They have taken away her Lord and she does not know where they placed Him. Would this stranger be able to tell her where He is? She would then take Him herself! An obviously preposterous proposition, but love is just like that. And He said to her: Mary!

In the upper room in Jerusalem the group of apostles are huddled together for fear of the Jews. Presently He is there in their midst. They are speechless with amazement. This must be a ghost! No, He assures them, not a ghost but "only Jesus," the same they had known and loved. His one anxiety is to convince them that all is well. Not a word about their defection of the other night! If you were looking on, you would be inclined to think that, somehow, He must not have even heard about it.

He consoles them on the seashore. Peter and John have been out all night and "when day was breaking Jesus stood on the beach." [2] As yet they do not recognize Him, but John, peering intently out over the side of the boat makes the discovery and at once tells Peter. They are cold after the long night and He has a fire to warm them. They are hungry and He has their breakfast cooked. The divine consoler was not insensible even to their material needs.

He joins two of them on the way to Emmaus. These had not yet heard the good news and His heart is gladdened at the prospect of giving it to them. Here too He "draws them out." Why were they so sad and dejected? Was it possible, came the rejoinder, that He had not heard about the extraordinary events that had happened in Jerusalem during the past few days? Concerning Jesus of Nazareth? He was mighty in word and work but the story of this man had ended in anti-climax. He had been crucified. He was dead and buried and their own high hopes had gone down with Him into the grave.

Sperabamus! We had hoped, but the sun has fallen out of our heaven. Not at all. He proceeds to prove to them that this Jesus of theirs had indeed fitted in perfectly with the descriptions and promises concerning the Messiah, as foretold by "Moses and all the prophets." How one longs for that exposition which opened their eyes and inflamed their hearts! "It is not the abundance of matter," writes Ignatius, "that fills and satisfies the soul, but to taste interiorly . . . to feel, to experience," not merely to be convinced intellectually. Their souls were "filled and satisfied" that day on the Emmaus road.

Loss of hope is most serious, for hope alone gives aim and purpose. Without hope our external work will not be quickened, our spiritual life will become a blind alley. The man with hope walks towards the light, even though it seems to be only a spark; without hope he has turned his back to the light and is in danger of wandering so far away as never to rediscover it. Men without hope are most dangerous, especially if they have no religion, for if the hope of happiness be excluded, morality disappears.

Our hopes are often enough mixed up with delusions;

time and training and experience rid us of these. At that stage it is very possible to give up all idealism, like the two disciples going to Emmaus, and settle down to a dog-in-the-manger existence. We let ourselves become "frustrated." We get cynical, hardened and disillusioned because life and people in actual fact are so very different from what we, in our dreamings, imagined them to be. We get a "raw deal" and smart under it and resolve to creep into our shell, make ourselves comfortable in it, quite sure of our own precious soul, and let the world outside go its way. No use trying! You will be as well thanked not to bother yourself! These are the hollow catchcries of the soul that gives up hope.

On the other hand the mistakes made by others, real or imagined, the "hard knocks" we get as we make our way through life, our "failures"—as we call them—can all conspire to throw us back on the sound principles established in the Exercises. It is especially at a period like the present one that we find magnificent opportunity to exercise ourselves in divine hope. In normal times, when there is peace and good will amongst men and nations, that act of confidence in God is less difficult.

But now—when the world is tottering, when on every side there is bloodshed, and homelessness, and hunger, and disease, and poverty and widespread famine; now—when men's minds seem obsessed with one only idea, how to seize and hold and extend power, regardless that millions must suffer death and ruin in the process; now—when God is ignored, or flagrantly opposed by the vast majority of men, when the very notion of His existence is scoffed at, when His Church is visibly losing ground in many areas and is fighting for her very existence, when her rights are shamelessly violated everywhere; now, in a word, when the vices condemned by Christ are enthroned and worshiped and the altars of the true God are desecrated and thrown down in ruins; at such a time and in such apparent triumph of might over right the Catholic stands upright, unbending, in the midst of the wreckage and makes use of his opportunity to affirm to himself and to the whole world the unfailing hope that with steady beat throbs all the while in his heart.

In spite of all appearances to the contrary I firmly believe that my God is watching over me individually and over the entire human race collectively. I believe that not a shot is fired, not a wound received, not a prayer whispered, not a sigh heaved, not a tear shed, not a thought, however flashing, conceived in any human mind, but my God knows all about it.

I believe that in some way which I do not profess to understand this frightful outburst of impiety is going ultimately to contribute to God's glory. I believe that the plague of war and pestilence will spread only where He permits it to spread. I believe that He will defend and spare those places and persons whom His Providence sees fit to defend and to spare. I know that nothing can happen to nations or to individuals except what He allows to happen to them. In a word, the dark days which make the cynic sneer at His Providence, the unintelligible happenings which make him smile patronizingly at my credulity, serve to consolidate my confidence in the all-knowing, all-directing guidance of my God. Not a sparrow falls to the ground without His knowledge. I know in whom I have trusted.

Sperabamus! What an assurance I would have in the

midst of the storm if I could be quite certain that His hand was indeed at the helm! What an immense comfort if I could be sure that He will steer the boat through the blackness of this night back into the full light of day! The world is steeped in darkness, Pope Pius XII told us, because men have re-crucified Christ. But I know that a rift was made in the heavy clouds that hung over Calvary and in the blaze of the Easter sunshine there stood revealed the radiant figure of Jesus triumphant. This is the spirit of the fourth week.

Life is a journey and often my bark is beaten upon by the waves and the danger of destruction seems imminent. But it is precisely when the waters rise mountains high that my hope in Him increases. *Sperabamus!* Small thanks to believe and trust Him when faith and hope are supported powerfully by external events. No great courage is demanded to row when the tide is with you, and a pleasant breeze is behind you, and the bright summer sun smiles down its cheering radiance upon you. But it takes grit to bare your arms and pull might and main against a strong current. It takes a man, or manly courage, to hold your own, and even advance, when the storm is howling on every side all around. It takes pluck to smile and keep up your spirits when the night is steeped in darkness and wise men tell you they can detect not a ray of hope.

That is why a Catholic needs to be, at all times but particularly today, not just good enough, but a hero. "Did not the Christ have to suffer these things"—it was His question on the Emmaus road—"before entering into his glory?" [3] Good Friday is the necessary prelude to Easter Sunday. Storms at sea happen every other day, but as I lean in terror over the side of the boat, grasping with both hands the railing while the deck sways up and down, I peer out into the darkness and on the shore I can still discern the figure, unaltered and unalterable, "Jesus Christ is the same yesterday and today, and yes, forever." [4]

XXIV

THE CLIMAX IS LOVE

AS the month's retreat draws to a close Ignatius directs
the prayerful attention of his exercitant to the mountain of divine love. He would have him first stand back
and view it in its sheer splendor and then he would invite
him to climb high up to the very summit and breathe into
his lungs the invigorating air to be found at the top. When
the retreat is finished and he goes back again to the val-
leys, let him carry away with him the constant memory
of the atmosphere enjoyed up here, for henceforth love
must be the driving force in every detail of his life.
"Whether it be question of washing a dish," writes Archbishop Goodier, "or solving the most abstruse scientific
problem, all is done for the King and the Kingdom."

Never consent to accept the caricature of Ignatius that
presents him as a loveless ascetic, insisting sternly on rigid
military obedience, efficient, inhuman, stoic in his strength
to endure. Never believe that he crushed the personality
of a man in giving him the Exercises or destroyed his individuality in molding him to his Order. "To purge out
all that is base in man," writes Father Thomas Burke, the
celebrated Dominican, "to give him entire dominion over
his senses and appetites, to raise his mind to loftiest
thoughts and fill his soul with highest aspirations, to form
his will in accordance with the noblest motives and pur-

poses; all this is not to destroy his individual character or personality but to develop and elevate it.

"And if in this process of development and elevation a number of men conform themselves to some high type of excellence, so as to become like each other in their common likeness to their type or model, this is not destroying that individuality which is sacred and must be respected, but rather directing its powers and shaping it to the highest and fairest. Well did St. Ignatius know this, and whilst destroying in his children all that was imperfect and base, he most carefully respected and reverently fostered the personal character and gifts of each man, so that in no Order in the Church is there a greater freedom and diversity of personal character, nor a wiser application and development of natural gifts than in the Society of Jesus."

Love is over all his rulings and directions. Much is written on his insistence on obedience but perhaps not enough stress has been laid on the truth that authority, in the exercise of it and in submissiveness to it, must be vivified by love. Subjects are to love Christ in every Superior. Superiors must imitate the kindness, sweetness, and charity of Jesus Christ our Lord, whom they too recognize in their sons. They should be chary of multiplying regulations and when they have to give an order let them as far as possible couch it more as a suggestion or recommendation rather than as a direct command. It was only with difficulty that Ignatius himself could be prevailed upon to write rules and constitutions for his sons. Little would suffice here, provided their hearts' love was centered on Jesus Christ. Thus "the interior law of charity and love, which the Holy Ghost is wont to write in the heart" is of immeasurably more value than any external constitutions. Still he did draw up some norms for their guidance, being moved to do so "by the sweet disposition of divine Providence."

Poverty must be practised because it is loved as a mother. Humility will never be learned until the soul be schooled to a love of humiliations. And his very first mention of love in the Exercises is in a meditation where we should, intelligibly enough, never think of looking for it —the meditation on hell. The object of thinking about hell is to inspire fear of God's judgments. But, be it well noted, for Ignatius fear is an emergency motive only, to fall back upon "if ever the love of God should grow cold in my heart."

Ignatius loved with a deep and lasting affection. His face would glow with love when he met another, for in him he saw Christ Himself. And he himself was greatly loved. Xavier would write him letters from India and China flowing over with a wealth of affection, and would go down on his knees and remain kneeling while reading what Ignatius wrote back in reply. Ribedeneira, a lively young novice, after a few days' absence suddenly burst into the sacristy one morning on his return home and threw his arms around Ignatius who was vesting for Mass. Laynez, one of his first companions, and Polanco, his trusted secretary, although consistently treated by him with apparent harshness, never wavered in the love and veneration they bore him.

So it is not surprising that before he lets his exercitant go, the saint will lay much emphasis on love, "the fulfilling of the law." His disciple has finished the Exercises, but Ignatius introduces him to a "Contemplation for Ob-

taining Divine Love," all on its own outside the retreat.
Like a stately mansion set in its own grounds, or like a
city seated on a high hill, it holds treasures which he must
not fail to inspect. Indeed the saint is loath to have him
leave until he has not only seen and admired, but actually
made his own, much of what he discovers of the wealth
contained; until he realizes that however much he may
have found here and however much he may carry away,
much still remains to be uncovered, and its value duly
appraised.

Every detail of the structure, as raised up by the saint,
is arresting to detain the soul. In even the setting and in-
troduction of his "contemplation" there is already an
abundance of material for a prayer that enkindles love of
God and is itself intensified according as love increases.
Here once more the sound advice he gave us so often
needs to be recalled—that we should not aim at fitting in
all his points, but should rest where we find fruit. The
purpose of the contemplation is not to confuse the soul
with too many ideas but rather to ensure that it come
down from the mountain on fire with divine love, with
heart aflame, like another Moses walking down from
Sinai.

As we climb up the mountain, or if you like, as we halt
in the grounds before entering the mansion, he gives us
two principles by way of clarifying what he means by
love. Love, he says, shows itself by deeds rather than by
words. Assurances of the love borne to another are not by
any means to be despised. Holy Scripture abounds in such
protestations made by a loving God and they are a well
of inexhaustible consolation to the soul. But words might
be suspect unless they were supported by the deeds of

love. That divine love has magnificently stood this test will become more and more evident as the contemplation proceeds. But at this initial stage Ignatius would warn us against a sugary piety which stops short at mere emotionalism. Not, as he has already shown, that feelings are to be despised, nor the expressions of love they evoke to be condemned, but these feelings and expressions ring truest when they goad the lover to act. "If you know these things, blessed shall you be if you *do* them." [1]

The second principle Ignatius insists upon at the outset of his contemplation is that love consists in a mutual interchange of gifts between those who love. Love seeks not what it can get from the person loved, but what it can give. "God so loved the world that he *gave* his only-begotten Son" [2] and the Son's supreme proof of love was seen when "bowing his head he *gave up* his spirit." [3] "Greater love than this no one has, that one lay down his life for his friends." [4]

Perfect love in this life is very rare. Motives of self-interest nearly always obtrude themselves. It may be suggested that the love of friendship is the highest type of love, because here there is perfect equality between those who love. Conjugal love and filial love and parental love postulate obedience, superiority, so that the two persons love at different levels. But in the love between friends there are no such inequalities, or if they do exist they tend to diminish and finally to disappear. And it is to the love of intimate friendship that God urges the soul! "No longer do I call you servants . . . but I have called you friends." [5] And why? Precisely because "all things that I have heard from my Father, I have made known to you." [6] There are to be no secrets henceforth between Him and them. He

is making them "coequals" with Himself, insofar as that
is possible through the grace He gives them.

This love of friendship, then, tends to become greater
and stronger according as He and the soul each give in
larger measure to the other. A gift is the proof and the
symbol of love. But a very important distinction is necessary when the two who love each other are God and the
soul. For in this case the soul has nothing of its own.
"What hast thou that thou hast not received?" [7]

A poor man owes me two dollars. Somebody sends me
ten dollars and tells me he wants it to be passed on to a
deserving family. No one I know could be more deserving than my needy friend so I give him the ten dollars as
a gift. If now he returns and hands me back two, has he
discharged his debt to me? Yes, for I made no sort of
stipulation. The money I gave him was his, but only because I gave it, and without it, let me suppose, he never
could have paid me back.

This is just our own position in the sight of God. We
present ourselves before Him in the rags of our sins; He
loads us with gifts because love wants to give. We are
now capable of giving but only because He made it possible for us. Hence the question is: *"Quid retribuam?*
What shall I give *back* to this most munificent Lover for
all that He has given to me?" Hence the soul is always
hopelessly in debt. None realize this with such agonizing
acuteness as the saints. In the competition in giving between Him and the loving soul He wins every time—must
win, refuses to allow Himself to be beaten.

XXV

APPRECIATION

THIS, then, is the final theme proposed for the exercitant's prayerful contemplation—the love of friendship between God and the soul; God loving the soul and proving His love by the giving of gifts; the soul reaching out in love to God, and trying in its helplessness and feebleness to show evidence of its sincerity by at least giving back what it has first had to receive. Let not the soul be bewildered at the sight of its insufficiency. Its love can be genuine because He has enriched its poverty. Nor need it imagine its love to be defective even if it feels no great warmth of affection. Love proves itself by deeds rather than by words. True love of God therefore is quite consistent with dryness of spirit, with feelings of aversion or disgust or weariness.

With these ideas as background, St. Ignatius in his "composition of place" urges the exercitant to stand steadily on this pinnacle, and from this high eminence try to penetrate with his gaze into heaven. The Mother of God is here, and angels and saints, "a great multitude which no man could number" [1] ranged before the throne of God. Steep your mind and heart, he advises, in this astounding fact, that all these are interceding for *you*. They are, each one individually and all of them collectively, deeply concerned about you. These are your friends. These are the members of God's great family to which you also belong. They look out eagerly for you to arrive. In the meantime they pray incessantly for you, that your journey may be safely made, that you may side-step the dangers and fill with the deeds of love each day and each night, every hour and every moment.

He touches here on the entrancing doctrine of the Communion of Saints. "God does not demand," writes Msgr. Scheeben, in his *Glories of Divine Grace*, "that we offer none but our own gifts. He accepts the good works of others in our name, if we unite ourselves with them and offer up their holy actions with the desire to perform the same works for His glory, and that being impossible, to glorify Him becomingly at least by offering these works. Thus you may offer up to God all the good works which have been performed from the beginning of the world, not only by the saints, the apostles, martyrs, confessors and virgins, not only by the angels, but also by the Blessed Virgin Mary and by Jesus Christ Himself.

"You may adore God with the adoration of His own incarnate Son and of all the saints, praise Him with their praise, love Him with their love, render thanks to Him with their thanks, pray to Him with their petitions, and suffer for Him with their patience. You may rejoice that they have served God with such love and devotion, and offer up this faithful service in atonement for your neglect and indolence. In this manner you may participate in the fruit of all these numerous and perfect works, and secure a higher degree of God's pleasure.

"But what an inexhaustible treasure have you then found for the increase of grace within you! How easy it is then for you to be enriched with grace daily and hourly, without any other trouble but the recollection that you may make this offering a hundred times every day without neglecting in the least your business and daily labor!"

In this atmosphere of "at-homeness" with saints and angels, with our Lord and His blessed Mother, St. Ignatius wants us to breathe. But is his supposition, perhaps, not somewhat farfetched, that all these are "interceding for me?" What am I—an insignificant drop from the gigantic ocean of humanity that has been rolling towards the shore of eternity for perhaps millions of years, that will continue to flow for only God knows how many centuries still? What am I compared with all heaven, the nine choirs of angels and the innumerable souls redeemed and saved? But I am yet a cell in the Mystical Body contributing, therefore, if I am in health, to the well-being of the whole organism.

That God be known and loved and served, this is the one all-consuming desire of the souls in heaven. Now they know that the exercitant, if he tries consistently to live the Exercises during the rest of his life, must of necessity be a most potent instrument for the salvation and the sanctification of souls. When they lived amongst us on earth, where at best we see truth so confusedly, we know that the saints were tireless, utterly self-forgetting, in exercise of the zeal that consumed them. Is it not reasonable to suppose, now that they see God face to face, now that they realize the value and beauty and destiny of each soul, that their desires have become more vehement and the intensity of their prayers more pressing? "I see myself standing before angels and saints, who are interceding for me." It is a truth to impart courage. It is a fact which cannot but increase in me my sense of responsibility.

Still here on the threshold let the exercitant beg for an
"internal knowledge" of so many and so great gifts which
God has given him, so that in the clear light of recogni-
tion he may be moved to love and serve His divine majesty
in all things. St. Ignatius is very fond of that word "internal." Here it seems to imply, not a mere factual knowledge, not a mere cataloguing of gifts received. He would
have the recipient dig deep down and learn experimen-
tally, by what he will feel and realize, the full significance
of the giving.

For the giver is God and the recipient is the insignificant creature, who has not only nothing good of his own,
but has repeatedly squandered God's gifts by sin. That
God should deign even to notice the presence of such a
creature is already high honor. That God should bestow
even a trinket on such a creature is already an entirely
undeserved sign of friendship. But that He should offer
gifts of immeasurable value, not offer them only but
eagerly press their acceptance on the sinner, that He
should offer the gift of intimate friendship with Himself,
not merely permitting the sinner's love, not tolerating it
only, but actually commanding it, saying: thou *shalt* love
—all this is overwhelming, and it is this Ignatius would
seem to have in mind when he bids his exercitant implore
"internal knowledge," keenly felt appreciation.

Some such realization the Baptist had of the chasm
separating his nothingness from the perfection found in
Christ. "It is I who ought to be baptized by thee, and dost
thou come to me?" [2] That God should inundate the soul,
and such a soul, with gifts; that these gifts, of their nature,
are in themselves so precious; that God implores the sinner to take them; all this, if realized, must produce a sense

of embarrassment, a confusedness, a genuine humility which is the soil most conducive to the growth and perfecting of love. "The most perfect discipline of human nature, the most effectual destruction of every selfish impulse, is attained by concentrating the whole attention upon God and the things of God, and upon all else in reference to God. ... This concentration upon God is the core and center of self-immolation, and leaves no place for the subtlest and most imperceptible movement of self-love or self-seeking. The *mind* thinks only of God; the *memory* is filled with Him; the *will* is one with His." (*Heavenly Converse*, by a Poor Clare Colletine.)

XXVI

TAKE AND RECEIVE

WE have to *begin* to love God from the motive of gratitude. But even supposing He had established no claim on our gratitude by giving gifts to us personally, it would still remain true that He is infinitely good in Himself, and to be loved therefore for this reason. In point of fact, He gives with lavish hand "good measure, pressed down, shaken together, [and] running over." [1] He is continually giving, lending us His own power, as it were; man is lord of creation, which in a true sense belongs to him, for it is man's privilege and duty to administer it so that it be used to give the fullest measure possible of glory to the Creator.

God is giving always. He is like the sun in the universality of His giving, but, unlike the sun He cannot injure, though perverse man can thwart Him. Ignatius begins the main section of his contemplation by asking his exercitant to stand back and make a survey or catalogue of God's gifts to himself. Should he ever feel depressed, it should be enough to restore him to put to himself the question: *What has God done for me?* A serious attempt to set down the answer, and depression, the saint believes, must fall off like a shroud. How could it coexist with an "internal knowledge" of the truth that the soul is loved by God, and that gifts of God—in proof of that love—are strewn along his way "like sands upon the great sea-shore"?

There are first the gifts he shares in common with all men. The fact of his being, the fact that he exists—the necessary presupposition to every other gift—he owes to the Creator who drew him forth from nothingness in the first instance. God chose him, singled him out from a number of others who might be considered as competitors for existence. He must know himself as God's preference, loved by Him with an everlasting love. And the number of "competitors," what is it? Why, the number of possible creatures assembled before the eyes of the Creator is infinite, without limit, without possibility of increase. So any soul whom He draws forth and enriches with the gift of actual living, must know itself to be God's special preference. An infinite number are rejected and it is chosen. The very gift of creation is already in itself a vocation.

For this one gift alone what could be an adequate return? *Quid retribuam?* If this alone were the one item on his list, the exercitant might well believe that whatever he gives, or whatever he says, or whatever he tries to do to express the love he owes is no more than a negligibly tiny portion of his debt. Creation alone would claim forever from him the consecration to God of all his faculties, so admirably formulated in the prayer of Ignatius:

"Take, O Lord, and receive, my whole liberty, my memory, my understanding, my whole will, whatever I have and possess. Thou hast given all these things to me; to Thee, O Lord, I restore them. All are Thine. Dispose of them in whatever manner Thou willest. Give me Thy love and Thy grace. With these I am rich enough and have nothing more to ask."

This is the acme of the spiritual life. The person who is prepared to live thus can go no further in the work of "disposing his soul" for whatever designs God may have on it. This prayer has been described as a synthesis of the whole teaching of St. John of the Cross. I owe it to God in justice; I owe it to Him in love; I owe it to Him absolutely, for the gift of creation; I would owe it for this one benefit alone, even supposing there were none other.

But the catalogue is far from being completed. Having created me, God must now continue to uphold me in existence from one second to the next. We depend on God much more absolutely than a man's shadow depends on the man, or the reflection in the mirror depends on the person who stands before it. This "conservation" of me on God's part might be compared to an endless series of creations. With every breath I draw, with every beat of my heart, I contract new obligations of love to Him. If my debt for the act by which He created me in the first instance was so great, it is now steadily and consistently mounting. I was insolvent before. To what heights have my obligations risen now—and they are increasing every moment!

St. Augustine has a prayer which might aptly be joined in this place with the prayer of St. Ignatius: "Take my heart, O Lord, for I cannot give it to Thee. Keep my heart, O Lord, for I cannot keep it for Thee. Send me any cross, O Lord, which may keep me subject to Thy cross, and save me in spite of myself!"

There is still the gift of "concurrence." My divine Lover does not merely preserve me, as He holds together, for instance, the elements in the chair upon which I sit. He has given me faculties, a mind to think and to reason, a will to love; He has given me power to move from one place to another, power to see, and speak, and laugh, and weep. But whenever I make any use of these gifts, even in the most passing manner, I need imperatively cooperation from Him. "Without me you can do nothing." [2] Never was a truth expressed with more literal exactitude. "God," it has been said, "is not only the Father of His creatures, but their Mother too."

To illustrate how deep my indebtedness now is, let me make here in His presence an act of gratitude. But even for that very act of gratitude I depend completely on Him. So I now owe Him another, and another, and yet another. I can never hope to catch up and discharge what I incur. The series is infinite. Even the saints, perhaps especially the saints, are vividly and perpetually conscious that whatever they give, whatever they do, even when their giving and their doing demand heroism, the contest must ever remain hopeless in their relations with a lover like this Lover.

Creation, conservation, concurrence, not yet is the full story told of the gifts received in common with the rest of mankind. For the world which God had "so" loved attempted in its madness to enthrone man in God's place. Sin raised its ugly head, unbridled passion goaded the world, God's world, to rebellion. God the Lover in face of such ingratitude continued to give gifts to men. Grace He had given wondrously to Adam, but to restore it after it had been wantonly abused was a more wondrous deed of love still. "O God," prays the priest at Mass, "who didst marvelously establish man's dignity, and in still

more marvelous manner didst restore it, grant to us by
the mystery of this water and wine, to be made the sharers
in the divinity of Him who deigned to become a sharer
of our human nature."

One might think we were somehow necessary to Him,
that somehow He stood in need of what we could give
Him, so persistently does He pursue us with His gifts!

Over and above all these proofs of His love, which I
hold in common with all men, there are also the gifts
lavished on me personally. To begin with there is this
very knowledge itself I have of Him and of His truth,
while the majority of mankind is groping in error. *What
has God done for me?* There are the blessings I am conscious of,—my Catholic education, the sacraments I have
received, the innumerable times He has forgiven me my
sins, the friends I have made, the kindnesses I have experienced, my successes in business, the happiness I find in
the particular walk of life that is mine.

Then there are the blessings I do not know and never
shall know, till I meet Him in heaven. What a revelation
it will be when in the light of His divine countenance I
shall see so differently what I now call failure and misfor-
tunes! "For those who love God all things work together
unto good." [3] A man at the risk of his life snatches a child
of three just in the nick of time from an oncoming truck.
The child has not the sense to understand what it owes
him; it may even be indignant and angry that he has
treated it roughly. In eternity I shall see that many of the
trials of which I complained so bitterly should have been
set down rather among the catalogue of blessings—sickness, loneliness, financial loss, frustration.

Let any one of these magnificent truths sink in, counsels Ignatius. You will never exhaust the force of any single one of them, the energy lying latent in them, to stir up your love. Insofar as friendship is tested by giving, God's friendship has stood the test wonderfully. From the first page of the Exercises their author has insisted that life has one only purpose, the loving, unquestioning, un-qualified bowing down of the creature before the Creator, of the son before the Father, in praise, in reverence, in service. This final contemplation is the apex of the same teaching. No soul can advance farther. The prayer "Take and Receive" was first spoken by Mary, and after Mary by Christ her Son. Mary said: "Be it done to me according to thy word!" [4] In Gethsemani Jesus cried out to His Father, and the words He spoke were: "Not my will, but thine be done!" [5]

XXVII

"THE BETTER GIFTS"

YOUR friend will appreciate a valuable gift you send to him by mail. But if you knock at his door yourself, and with your own hands present it to him, you will certainly enhance its value in his eyes. If you give a poor man a generous alms but accompany your action with loud complaints of his importunity, you will, as we say, "take the good out" of what you give. He gives twice over who gives graciously, and God Himself loves the cheerful giver.

The mere catalogue of God's gifts is awe-inspiring to examine, and yet how close and prolonged soever the scrutiny be, we can never reach at anything more than an inkling of the love that prompts them. It would be much had He given us what Ignatius has outlined for us, and had then, so to say, allowed us to carry on ourselves from there. A father who brings home a toy for his child and sends him off to play with it while he settles down to smoke his pipe and read in his armchair, surely shows a measure of love for his child. But everyone sees how greater the love is if the father, tired perhaps after a hard day, forgets his weariness to play with the child, to get on his knees and demonstrate how the toy "works," and to answer the innumerable queries which pour forth from the youngster's fertile imagination.

Much depends on the manner of giving. When the lover or the friend accompanies his giving with the "personal touch," he gives with the gift himself also. The divine lover will not let Himself be outdone here. He remains in the very midst of His creation. His presence in inanimate nature is shown by the fact that He keeps it in existence. He is the gardener under whose care flowers and trees spring to life. He is the shepherd who gives life, in the natural order, to His sheep and to the whole animal world. His presence and power are discernible in the fly dashing against the window pane not less than in the lion parading in the jungle.

But in man His presence transforms the human soul into His temple. All the gifts already poured out on man have not succeeded in satisfying the love of this lover. He must abide in man's soul, settling down there permanently. "If anyone love me ... my Father will love him, and we will come to him and make our abode with him." [1] This is the work of grace in the soul. In every man there is something which only the infinite can fill. That is why man is happy only insofar as he tries to be more than man. This tendency is satisfied in the Incarnation—God becoming man and lifting man up to share in His Godhead, to share in a real way in the divine nature and become in fact God's very son by adoption.

Thus, as Ignatius would say, "God dwells in His gifts." "Rejoice and praise, O thou habitation of Sion, for great is he that is in the midst of thee, the Holy One of Israel." [2] "In him we live and move and have our being." [3] As Mary found Him in the temple, the exercitant must seek and find Him in the temple of his own soul. Mary and Joseph sought Him "sorrowing" and there is something sadly lacking in the spiritual life of one who never, or at only rare intervals, finds Him in the temple of the soul. "Master, where dwellest thou?" [4] All creation is the rustle of His garment.

Nor may we omit from our catalogue His dwelling in our midst in the Holy Eucharist. An omnipotent lover is here taxing His powers so as to remove every possible vestige of doubt from our minds regarding the depth and truth of the love He bears us.

Through all these gifts He designs to work out His purposes. What tools are to a skilled workman; what brushes and paints are to the artist; what books are to the student; what bricks and mortar are to the builder; what instruments are to the surgeon, this is what every second of time, and every event that happens in time, is in the hands of the divine lover. What He ordains or permits, He utilizes for the furthering of His glory and the growth of grace, or the sowing of grace, or the restoring of grace if it be lost, in the souls of men.

These are the bracing truths Ignatius talks about to his exercitant as they both stand contemplating together the view of life that stretches out far and wide beneath their feet from the mountain of love.

The summing up of it all is that "One there is who is good, and he is God." [5] Whatever we find that is lovable or beautiful in our world is no more than a reflection of the beauty or lovableness of which the source is God. "Every good gift and every perfect gift," writes St. James in the first chapter of his epistle, "is from above, coming down from the Father of lights, with whom there is no change nor shadow of alteration." [6] "The heavens declare the glory of God and the firmament proclaims his handiwork." [7]

As we make our way through life we encounter people whose character readily wins our admiration and our love. They are conscientious, ready to help—and with a willing smile—wherever there is need. Habitually cheerful themselves they seem to spread sunshine all around. Rarely do they permit themselves a word of censure, though they are adepts at finding excuses for those who err. Above all they are twenty-four-hour-a-day Catholics, and it is their knowledge of their faith and their practical love of it, and their consistent loyalty to its principles, that exercise so formative an influence in developing in them a character so universally attractive.

Of St. Francis de Sales it was said: "What must God be like, if the Bishop of Geneva is so lovable?"

Outside the household of the faith too there are many, very many, whose innate nobility of conduct cannot fail to win our love. We find it hard probably to suppress a feeling of regret that persons like these, whose educated minds would find such satisfying assurance in the Catholic Faith, are deprived, seemingly through no fault of their own, of this inestimable teaching.

All this natural goodness in men, and all the supernatural virtue produced in them by grace, comes down from the Father of lights. All the truly lovable qualities that have ever shone in the fairest specimens of our human race, if added together and multiplied a thousand times, argue to the ravishing beauty of the infinite God. Now if in this valley of tears we find in man so much that captivates and inspires, here where we are handicapped by so many obstacles to a virtuous life, where

greed so easily consumes us, where passion is ever ready
to blind our eyes and harden our hearts—if, with all this
to oppose them, men can yet rise to such heights of virtue,
what will they be hereafter?

You have often thrilled to the beauty of a summer day
with glorious sunshine in a blue sky that was filled with
music. You have sat enthralled, mesmerized it might
seem, as with closed eyes you drank into your soul the
cadences of some symphony orchestra. There is beauty
all around, in the snow-capped mountains, in the lilies
of the field, in the peace of the silent valley, in art and
literature, in the golden sunset, in the leaves falling to
the ground in autumn.

But this world is our land of exile. This is a mere halting
place on our journey home. For many it is a prison cell
where sickness and poverty and hunger are like manacles
of steel binding them hand and foot. Still even here there
is so much to cheer and gladden us, the most sorely tried
of us, at least from time to time. If the Creator has spread
abroad such beauty here, if the divine Artist has expended
so much skill in coloring the walls that are so soon to
crumble away, what care must He have exercised, and
with what results, when the task before Him was to build
a home—not a mere resting place—but a home for the sons
and daughters He loves, where He will wipe away all
tears from their eyes, and God shall be all in all! "And
the city has no need of the sun or the moon to shine upon
it. For the glory of God lights it up, and the Lamb is the
lamp thereof." [8]

What can a man in a dark room know of the masterful
brilliance of the sun, if he must judge only from a sickly
ray penetrating through a crevice in the shutter? What

notion can he form of the limitless expanse of sea from the few drops of water beating on his window? What estimate can you have of the style and power of a literary masterpiece if all you have to go by is the crude childish essay put together by the author when he was aged four?

Yet it is to be asserted that the knowledge these give —the straggling sun ray, the drop of water, or the sprawling page covered with ink blots—of the source of their greatness, is immeasurably more comprehensive than what we can learn of God from His creation. He surpasses infinitely the wildest flights of our imagination. "*Quantum potes, tantum aude, quia major omni laude, nec laudare sufficis.* Let your praise of Him multiply as much as you possibly can; employ the most daring expressions to describe Him; He is beyond all praise, He is greater and more beautiful and more exalted than you will ever find words in which to tell." "But as it is written: 'Eye has not seen, nor ear heard, nor has it entered into the heart of man, what things God has prepared for those that love him.' " [9]

"God is love." [10] "More than this we need not add; let the last word be: he is all in all!" [11]

XXVIII

THINKING WITH
THE CHURCH

FOR Ignatius "the Church was the creation of the Holy Ghost, through which the Redeemer would be present in all ages, to all mankind. . . . His emphasis on the authority of the Church itself is not the effect of any love of authority as such, but of his conviction that through the Church's authority man has access to the wisdom and goodness of God. . . . I am concerned with those Catholics who would minimize the Church's claim to speak authoritatively on temporal matters where the moral conscience is concerned. . . ."

The very last page of the Exercises describes the Catholic mentality toward the teachings of the Church. Like so much else in the book it can be aptly applied to us who are living four hundred years after it was written. St. Ignatius embodies what he wants to tell us in a series of eighteen rules, which deal with *faith, discipline,* and *devotion.*

Faith. Faith is belief in a given truth on the word of another. Divine Faith is belief in revealed truth because God has revealed it. There are three ways among others by which He can convey that truth to us. First He can come into the world and speak directly Himself, and this He did in the Incarnation. Secondly He can give us

His message in writing, guaranteeing its authenticity, and this is Sacred Scripture, written by men under His inspiration and therefore immune from error. Lastly He can establish a group of men, commission them to preach by word of mouth, to pass on to subsequent generations what they had heard from Him, promising them that He will be with them till the end of time to guide them aright.

This first group form the nucleus around which have developed the unnumbered millions who constitute the Catholic Church. "Between Christ our Lord, the Bridegroom," writes Ignatius, "and the Church His Bride, there is one and the same Spirit, who governs and directs us for the salvation of our souls, because our holy Mother the Church is ruled and governed by the same Spirit and our Lord who gave the Ten Commandments." This is the foundation of the love and obedience he expects for the Church from every right-minded Catholic. "To make sure of being right in all things, we ought always to hold by the principle that the white that I see I would believe to be black, if the hierarchical Church were so to rule."

The Church is never going to tell me to believe that white is black. The saint is merely emphasizing the absolute confidence I am to have in any decision of the Church. If she were to tell me some object was white which seemed to me to be black, so deeply rooted is my faith in her, that instinctively I assume that the mistake is on my side. It is worthwhile adding that the Church, before making a pronouncement, uses the utmost care in examining a question from every angle. An instance of this took place at the Council of Trent. On one single point of doctrine the Council held sixty-one General

Congregations and forty-four others, each occupying
from three to six hours. Three different drafts on the
point were drawn up, discussed word by word with
most painstaking scrutiny, and after all this were finally
rejected!

Even if she never claimed to be guided infallibly by
God, would it be very rash to yield implicit obedience
to the teachings of a Church that goes to such extraordinary lengths to safeguard herself against error?

Discipline. It is probable that our loyalty to the Church
is tested principally in matters of discipline which affect
us very nearly. She has definite rulings about mixed marriages, divorce, birth control, education, self-denial, secret societies, the reasons justifying war, or strikes, or
defiance of the lawfully constituted government of a
country. These rulings may often prove to be a severe
trial. A Catholic may chafe at certain decisions made by
local Church authority and be sorely tempted to give way
to sharp criticism or even open disobedience.

It is in such circumstances that the right Catholic mentality is reflected most perfectly. The mind is kept in that
attitude which seeks to defend "all the precepts of the
Church, ready to seek reasons for defending her and in
no way impugning her." Wherever a man in a position
to speak with her authority gives a ruling it is the hall-
mark of Catholicity to support it unquestioningly.

Suppose there is in actual fact some abuse of authority.
Suppose restrictions are imposed which irritate by their
seeming injustice? One reaction is to carp and criticize
such restrictions and the policy behind them, indiscrimi-
nately, before any audience willing to listen. Such criticism of any authority, Church or State, can lead to

nothing but discontent and bitterness; "it gives rise," says St. Ignatius, "to murmurs and scandals among the people. . . ." There are those who send letters of protest to the press, who denounce from public platforms, who never miss the chance to raise a sneer against authority. What do these effect?

St. Ignatius is not against fair criticism of authority, made in the right spirit and to the right persons. No reasonable Superior but will welcome this, for it is extremely useful to him to have the balanced views of his subordinates. When these are submitted in a spirit of charity, with the sincere desire for the common good, no sensible person can object.

Devotion. In the final section of these rules St. Ignatius bids us speak and commend prayer, the use of the sacraments, holy Mass, pilgrimages, the veneration of the saints, the building and adornment of churches.

An innovation he introduced into his Order was the omission of the Divine Office in choir. Jesuits say their Office in private. But it is quite certain that the saint loved the sacred ceremonies of the liturgy and this omission he approves of only because he would have his men free at any hour to be of service to their neighbor. He would rejoice at the restored Holy Week and at the widespread enthusiasm with which Catholics have welcomed it.

We have already set down some of his ideas about prayer, which has been well described by Père Petit, a French Jesuit, as "the barometer of the spiritual life."

He strongly advocates frequent Holy Communion, and again we know he would be the first to encourage all, priests and laity, to avail themselves of the vastly increased opportunities afforded by evening Mass and the new rules governing the Eucharistic fast.

He would have the exercitant "praise the ornaments and building of churches." We remember the splendid temple built by Solomon. *By God's own command* no expense was to be spared because the temple was to be the house of God and the gate of heaven. But Solomon's temple was a mere figure of the Catholic Church in which the Son of God abides all day and all night in the Real Presence. Any Catholic who has even a dim realization of what the Blessed Sacrament means will admit unquestioningly that if every stone in our churches were of pure gold they would still be unworthy of their most sublime purpose.

Especially appropriate for our day is the saint's reminder to uphold the practice of penance, "not only interior but also exterior." Pope Pius XII deplored the growing tendency in the Church to regard as obsolete "the virile penances of old." To this tendency the Vicar of Christ attributed in large measure the victories of communism. At Lourdes our Lady asked for "Penance, Penance, Penance." At Fatima she bids us say the Rosary, but she insists no less emphatically on the fact that our prayer must be seasoned with the spirit of self-sacrifice.

There is no "thinking with the Church" in the doctrine that would overlook the need of penance and maintain that nothing more than pure love is of value in God's sight. Love will not be pure unless it expresses itself in the deeds of a penitential life. "Every one of you who does not renounce all that he possesses, cannot be my disciple." [1] A love of ease and a tendency to multiply comforts may be defended on the grounds that it is sound common sense. But there is a common sense which ill accords with the foolishness of the cross.

"If thou reliest more on thine own reason than on the virtue that subjects to Jesus Christ, thou wilt seldom or hardly become an enlightened man. For God will have us wholly subject to Him, and to transcend all reason by an inflamed love." This sentiment of à Kempis, Ignatius would have endorsed warmly. This is clear from the manner in which one of his first disciples, probably Father Peter Ribadeneira, summed up the Ignatian ideal. Those aspiring to the realization of this ideal must be:

"Men crucified to the world and to whom the world itself is crucified, new men, I say, who have put off their own affections to put on Christ; dead to themselves to live to justice; who with St. Paul in labors, in watchings, in fastings, in chastity, in knowledge, in long-suffering, in sweetness, in the Holy Ghost, in charity unfeigned, in the word of truth, show themselves ministers of God, and by the armor of justice on the right hand and on the left, by honor and dishonor, by evil report and good report, by good success finally and ill success, press forward with giant strides to their heavenly country themselves, and, by all means possible and with all zeal, urge on others also, ever looking to God's greatest glory."

XXIX

EPILOGUE

THE Constitutions drawn up by Ignatius "anticipated as well as looked back," writes the Jesuit, Father George O'Neill. "May we not expect this wherever the Holy Spirit, 'the Giver of lights,' has been allowed to operate? The glorification of Christ the King was there centuries before Pius XI marked it out by appointing a new festival. The motto 'To restore all things in Christ' was as dear to the heart of Ignatius as to that of St. Pius X. Like Leo XIII Ignatius was eager for the thorough training of Catholics, especially of the clergy, in schools and seminaries, by means of the soundest theology and philosophy. And if our time rejoices to hail in Pius XI a 'Pope of the Missions,' surely Ignatius was a 'Saint of the Missions' for his own distracted sixteenth century!

"In his love of religious poverty, in his hatred of the mere suspicion of simony, Ignatius looked back to St. Francis of Assisi. In his appreciation of the preaching ministry and of intellectual weapons in the fight for religion he renewed the high traditions of St. Dominic. And if he could not emulate St. Benedict and the other monastic founders in their centralized devotion to the liturgy, yet he yielded this ground to them only with regret; he definitely ordered his followers to 'praise the chanting of hymns and psalms in the church, long devotions, and the celebration at fixed times of the Canonical Hours.'

"Is there anything more? The notable austerities, sack-cloth and bare feet, of hermits and monks, the prolonged contemplations and mystic exaltations of the silent recluses—such things could not be the subject of rules for an actively apostolic Society. But in his Exercises and in the spirit of his Rule Ignatius opens up unrestricted possibilities, and even invitations, as regards all these aspects and practices of Christian perfection. None is excluded; none is undervalued by the holy founder himself, nor by his most illustrious followers."

SCRIPTURAL QUOTATIONS

9. Ps. 18:13
10. Is. 1:2
11. Heb. 5:7
12. Apoc. 21:4, 5

CHAPTER XXI

1. I Cor. 12:11
2. I Cor. 15:41
3. I Cor. 3:2

CHAPTER XXII

1. John 16:22
2. Rom. 6:9
3. Rom. 6:4
4. I John 3:2
5. Phil. 4:4
6. Apoc. 4:11
7. Apoc. 5:12, 13

CHAPTER XXIII

1. II Cor. 12:2
2. John 21:4

3. Luke 24:26
4. Heb. 13:8

CHAPTER XXIV

1. John 13:17
2. John 3:16
3. John 19:30
4. John 15:13
5. John 15:15
6. John 15:15
7. I Cor. 4:7

CHAPTER XXV

1. Apoc. 7:9
2. Matth. 3:14

CHAPTER XXVI

1. Luke 6:38
2. John 15:5
3. Rom. 8:28

4. Luke 1:38
5. Luke 22:42

CHAPTER XXVII

1. John 14:23
2. Is. 12:6
3. Acts 17:28
4. John 1:38
5. Matth. 19:17
6. James 1:17
7. Ps. 18:1
8. Apoc. 21:23
9. I Cor. 2:9
10. I John 4:9
11. Sirach 43:28

CHAPTER XXVIII

1. Luke 14:33

Set up, printed and bound by Benziger Brothers, Inc., New York.